THE *Best Sex*

OF (MY LIFE

Confessions of A Sexual Purity Revolution

Lindsay Marsh Warren, MD

Author of *The Best Sex of My Life: a Guide to Purity*
and President of the Worth The Wait Revolution, Inc

ISBN: 978-1-4669-6025-1 (sc)
ISBN: 978-1-4669-6027-5 (hc)
ISBN: 978-1-4669-6026-8 (e)

Library of Congress Control Number: 2012923135

Trafford rev. 12/07/2012

 www.trafford.com

North America & international
toll-free: 1 888 232 4444 (USA & Canada)
phone: 250 383 6864 ♦ fax: 812 355 4082

Contents

Dedication

To my husband Gareth,
for always supporting me and allowing me to soar.
Thank you for leading our family to the next dimension . . .

Acknowledgements

I am very thankful for all of the support, encouragement and favor I have received during this project.

Special thanks to all of the special individuals who submitted a contribution to this book. I applaud your boldness and courage. I pray that many lives will be changed as a result of your confession. The confessions of this sexual purity revolution are REAL!

Special thanks to my editors, for making this book, an excellent book. Sam Carrington, Heavenly Beloved, Allysha Sneed, Tawana Burks and Gareth P. Warren: I am honored that you would help me accomplish this assignment.

Special thanks to Worth The Wait Revolution, Inc. To the Board of Directors, models, volunteers, and partners: I sincerely appreciate you giving of your lives to further the vision of "sexual purity with contemporary style and urban class". Long live the REVOLUTION!

Special thanks to my WordUp! College Outreach family. It is truly an honor to serve you all and watch you all grow and blossom into great people of purpose.

Special thanks to my Pastors, Drs. Michael and DeeDee Freeman and the Spirit Of Faith Christian Center family for teaching me the 'spirit of faith', and covering us with your wisdom and prayers. You guys rock!

Special thanks to my parents, Dr. Lonnie and Vivian Marsh II. I am grateful for every sacrifice, every hug, every kiss, every pat on the back, every word of encouragement and every tuition dollar paid. I am who I am, because of you.

Special thanks to my family: The Warren family, Marsh family, Tarver family, Lancelin family, Lee family, Tucker family and Walker family. I love you guys, dearly.

Special thanks to Elder Tim and Minister Danielle McLean. Thank you for being a family, to my family.

Super thanks to the Holy Spirit for inspiring this book. This idea came directly from Him, and I am excited about the lives that will be revolutionized as a result. All the glory and the honor belongs to God!

Introduction

The Best Sex of My Life: Confessions of a Sexual Purity Revolution is the second book, in *The Best Sex of My Life* Series. When I wrote my first book in 2006, I was finishing my anesthesiology residency at The George Washington University. In the same year, I turned thirty years old. An internal alarm of panic suddenly went off. How was I single, thirty, without a man, and without any prospects (that I really liked)? I was puzzled, confused, and curious about this major delay. The Lord spoke to me very clearly (in my heart), and said, "Lindsay, YOU ARE WORTH THE WAIT!!" Those simple, yet significant words changed the very course and direction of my life forever. The first "I AM WORTH THE WAIT" shirt was printed and quickly gained popularity. People began to ask me how they could get one of my shirts for themselves or loved ones, and in that moment, a clothing line was born. In July 2006, I celebrated my thirtieth birthday party with a launch of the newly founded *Worth The Wait Revolution Inc.*, the non-profit organization I was led to start. The launch consisted of the release and book signing of *The Best Sex of My Life: a Guide to Purity* (my first book), as well as the official launch of the "I AM WORTH THE WAIT" brand. Pre-teens, teenagers, college students, adult singles, supporters and friends gathered for the extravagant celebration. From that day in July 2006, non-profit organizations, high schools, colleges, ministries, mentoring organizations and the like, have supported the Revolution by graciously opening their doors to me, and making bulk purchases of books, shirts and other resources. The website, www.iamworththewait.com became the new home to the sexual purity movement, which was quickly gaining momentum and strong support. The Worth The Wait Revolution models, volunteers and I have travelled to many, many different places throughout the United States, and soon we will have open doors to go abroad with our message. I have been completely humbled and amazed to see the number of lives that have been impacted since the inception of the REVOLUTION.

Although, I continued to desire marriage and intimacy, I was determined to pursue my purpose. I recognized that July 2006 gave birth to a movement, a vision, a mission, and a great assignment. We expanded the outreach, by hosting an evening of elegance every February, called the Worth The Wait Revolution Gala. The Gala, being a substitute for the Valentine's Day blues, developed into an exquisite evening of dinner and dancing, but more importantly, our "Sexual Purity Real Conversations". These real, transparent conversations began to sharpen and focus the partnership of the REVOLUTION, and foster real change, as evidenced by changed lives. I openly shared about my freedom from masturbation and 'satisfaction without penetration'; while others shared about their freedom from pornography, homosexuality, poor choices, sexual abuse, and the like. Because of God's presence, each Worth The Wait Revolution Gala became a place of healing and restoration, for where the Spirit of the Lord is, there is liberty (2 Corinthians 3:17).

We expanded the outreach by conducting annual model calls to recruit for the clothing line and other Worth The Wait Revolution events. I would often teach the models, ". . . your life is a runway because people are watching your lifestyle wherever you go". The model calls grew and evolved over time, consisting of an application process, runway audition and interview. The annual Worth The Wait Revolution Runway Events allowed opportunities for models to be featured wearing the "I AM WORTH THE WAIT" brand, while sharing their own stories. I began a runway scene entitled, 'Confessions of a Revolution' because I wanted people to understand that sexual purity is possible for every age and every stage of life. This runway format became a very successful and impactful method to reach our audiences, because it celebrated victory over homosexuality, lust, perversion, abortion, promiscuity, sexual abuse, rape and other sexually immoral acts. The voices of this REVOLUTION needed to be heard then, and they need to be heard now. Many people have been hurt and are still hurting, as a result of bad choices, bad circumstances or even people with bad intentions. Regardless of how the hurt has come or where the hurt has come from, this book will bring healing, wholeness and restoration to your soul. We overcome by the blood of the Lamb and by the word of our testimony (Revelation 12:11)!

I believe that it is not a coincidence that you are reading this book. I believe that the words shared in this book will bring you real encouragement, real insight and real freedom. Do not allow your past to be the prison that keeps you from your bright future. I have been inspired to share even deeper things about my journey, while combining the journeys of other, to bring you to a place of wholeness: A new place of satisfaction, renewal and peace with God. I welcome you to challenge yourself to move to the next level of satisfaction, wholeness and completion.

I hated the feeling of condemnation that followed an episode of masturbation or an episode with an old boyfriend. I couldn't stand the fact that I could say I didn't have sex with a guy, but came so close to it that I felt the same level of guilt. I want you to be free from the condemnation of your past. Make a decision today, that just like those who are sharing in this very book, you too, will be able to make the necessary changes. Your life will not be the same after reading this book. You will be inspired to know your worth and your value, in a greater way. Males and females alike, I encourage you to embrace the testimonies shared and to learn from the lives of others.

Jesus said, "This day, salvation has come to your house" (Luke 19:9). However, I am saying to you, this day, the REVOLUTION has come to your house and your life will never ever be the same!!

My Confession

Virgin? At first they really didn't believe me. Could I really be a 30+ year old virgin? Many people were curious. How could you be attractive and still be a virgin? How could you be successful and still be a virgin? How could you be 'normal' and still be a virgin? The "Worth The Wait" lady, was my nickname for a while. Travelling throughout the country with a message of sexual purity, a book entitled, *The Best Sex of My Life: a guide to purity*, and a desire to see this generation make better sexual choices; people's lives began to change and become impacted by the REVOLUTION. Worth The Wait Revolution began hosting annual Runway Events in 2006 and Annual Galas in 2008, with the theme of *"sexual purity with contemporary style and urban class"*. The face of abstinence, celibacy and purity was in the process of being completely revamped. I began to openly and transparently share my journey toward sexual purity; the good, the bad and the not-so-good. Although I was a virgin, I had participated in various acts that were unacceptable or displeasing to the Lord, such as masturbation, humping, "bumpin & grindin", and the like. I had been exposed to pornography as a child. I had my experience of 'touching' and playing 'house' as a child. I made my life an open book. Yes, I was a virgin, and yes, I had made poor choices. However, through and by a real desire to please God, application of practical principals from the Word of God, and good spiritual leadership, I obtained victory. The Bible clearly states that ". . . we overcome by the blood of the Lamb and by the word of our testimony" (Revelation 12:11). I was inspired in 2006 to write my first book, so that through my testimony, others could be inspired to walk in sexual purity, regardless of their past encounters.

Now, I'm inspired to write this book because there are many stories of victory and great triumph to be told. The Worth The Wait Revolution has impacted the lives of thousands and very soon, millions, through our books, DVDs, audio books, Runway Events, Galas, Sexual Purity Real Conversations and more. I'm very humbled and thankful to God for being chosen to represent this REVOLUTION for such a time as this.

Unfortunately, in 2011 statistics from the Centers for Disease Control and Prevention (CDC) revealed that 70% of African-American children are born to unwed parents and moreover, the CDC reports that in 2012, one-half of the 19 million new STD cases will occur among those from ages 15-24. African-Americans are the highest at risk. In spite of those statistics, God is raising us up as a new standard. Isaiah 59:19 states, "When the enemy shall come in like a flood, the Spirit of the LORD shall lift up a *standard* against him." You and I are the standard! We have been called to be the standard in this generation. During a time when sexploitation, adultery, child pornography, homosexuality, same-sex marriage and perversion are flooding our culture, God has declared you and me to be the standard. He desires to 'lift up' those who choose to be a part of this sexual purity REVOLUTION. I believe you are reading this book, at this very moment because you sense the inward calling and assignment to be the 'salt and the light'. Jesus announced our identity, saying:

> "You are the salt of the earth: but if the salt has lost its flavor, wherewith shall it be salted? It is thenceforth good for nothing, but to be cast out, and to be trodden under foot of men. You are the light of the world. A city that is set on a hill cannot be hid. Neither do men light a candle and put it under a bushel, but on a candlestick. And, it gives light unto all that are in the house. Let your light so shine before men, that they may see your good works, and glorify your Father which is in heaven".
> Matthew 5:13-16 (NKJV)

The Message Bible truly brings this scripture to life. It reads:

> "Let me tell you why you are here. You're here to be salt-seasoning that brings out the God-flavors of this earth. If you lose your saltiness, how will people taste godliness? You've lost your usefulness and will end up in the garbage. Here's another way to put it: You're here to be light, bringing out the God-colors

in the world. God is not a secret to be kept. We're going public with this, as public as a city on a hill. If I make you light-bearers, you don't think I'm going to hide you under a bucket, do you? I'm putting you on a light stand. Now that I've put you there on a hilltop, on a light stand—shine! Keep open house; be generous with your lives. By opening up to others, you'll prompt people to open up with God, this generous Father in heaven".

Matthew 5: 13-16 (MSG)

Wow! Enough said!

MY DISTRACTIONS

Before I met my husband I was, at various times, preoccupied with other guys who I *thought*, were my husband. You know how we do, ladies! We RUN with it! If we think someone is our husband (ladies) or our wife (fellas), we RUN with it!! We jump in! Head first!! Have you ever heard of the movie, "He's Just Not That Into You"? Well, one particular guy was just not that into me. What a newsflash. Can you believe it? Me? Yes, me! As singles, I know we walk by faith but sometimes we get beyond the faith process and enter into foolishness and presumption. I regret wasting so much time, consumed by the 'idea' of relationships that proved to be fruitless. I was never physically involved with these guys, but I wish I could get back the time I spent on the phone calls, emails, text messages, planning and day-dreaming. Sometimes, we need to learn how to stop stalking people. (I've been there. Don't get mad at me. I love you and because I love you, I must tell you the truth. Real relationships do not require stalking on Facebook, Twitter or Instagram.)

Honestly, I'm so thankful that the Lord did not allow me to go down those paths, because sometimes the person that we envision to be 'the one' is quite frankly, 'the wrong one' on so many levels. They are totally wrong for our mission, wrong for our mandate and wrong for our spiritual maturity in Christ. Furthermore, if someone does not recognize your worth and value, they are not worthy of your time and affection. Sometimes, we are so blinded by our relationship ambitions that we fail to recognize when someone may not be a great match. We make excuses for their shortcomings, inconsistencies and lack of spiritual discipline. We rationalize their behaviors and ignore their 'issues'. This is an unhealthy, unacceptable way to navigate the relationship waters as a Christian that truly desires to please the Lord. The longer we waste time with the imposters and decoys, the longer we delay our true love.

OUR STORY

Well, of course I had 'the list' . . . every girl dreams of her husband. "He should be 6'3, handsome, charming, ambitious, caramel, athletic, brilliant, and wealthy, with a beautiful smile". Then, when I turned 18, my Pastors taught me that this list also needed to include spiritual things. That's when I revised 'my list' to include a born-again, spirit-filled, mature, purpose-driven man with a pure heart. I'd compromised on 'my list' in times past, only to discover impostors and distractions. God always had His best waiting for me, in Gareth.

I saw him on Super Bowl Sunday in February 2009 and I married him as a 34-year-old virgin on October 30, 2010. His name is Gareth P. Warren and he is my HUSBAND!! The Lord blessed me with an amazing, handsome, intelligent, ambitious, anointed man of God. A sexy man! I believed Psalms 37:4 during the season of my singleness. "Delight yourself also in the LORD: and He shall give you the desires of your heart." As destiny would have it, my husband read my first book, *The Best Sex of My Life: a Guide to Purity*, prior to us even becoming aware of one another's existence. I didn't know him and he didn't know me. He was given the book as a gift during the summer of 2008, from a mutual friend, Ms. Joy Stevenson, who is a wonderful woman we both adore. Of course, during this time of my life, I was conducting the ministry business of Worth The Wait Revolution, overseeing the college outreach "WordUp!" for my Pastor, and practicing anesthesiology by day. Life was busy, but I knew that my husband would cross my path in due season. So, Gareth walked into Spirit of Faith Christian Center on a Sunday evening, and sat in front of my mom. He was so handsome, and quite frankly, I loved his swag. Immediately, he caught my eye. Tall, broad shoulders, nice lips . . . I thought he was very attractive. "Who is he?" my mom asked out of curiosity. Just as curious, I replied, "I have no idea, but he is NICE."

I later learned that he was there to be a part of the baby dedication ceremony with the Joiner family. My family was there to be a part of the baby dedication ceremony for my niece. We didn't meet one another that evening at church, but we certainly took notice of one another. Ms. Joy Stevenson proceeded to play cupid and hook us up. She actually called me the next day and told me that Gareth was a great guy, originally from Texas. She spoke very highly of him, stating his accolades, and how she thought we might make a perfect fit for one another. She told me that he worked in corporate finance for a prestigious Fortune 500 company, he had recently purchased a home in Baltimore, and that he was single. Furthermore, she went on to tell me that she had given him my book as a gift, the book changed his life, and he was now walking in sexual purity. Wow! So, that meant he already knew how I felt on many levels regarding love, intimacy and relationships. How awesome! Gareth signed the 'sexual purity confession covenant' located in the back of *The Best Sex of My Life: a Guide to Purity*, before we even knew one another. It's amazing to think about, but the Lord used my very own book to minister sexual purity to my future husband. Wow! This is why it is so critical to obey God, in all things. If He tells you to write a book, write it. If He tells you to go back to school, do it. If He tells you to volunteer your services for a certain cause, obey him. He has our best interest in mind, and desires to properly position us for our destiny. You will meet your future spouse on the pathway of purpose, which is directly connected to the pathway of obedience.

Eventually, Ms. Joy convinced me that I needed to check him out. She also convinced him that he needed to reach out to me. Within a few days Gareth emailed me through the Worth The Wait Revolution website, joined the Worth The Wait Revolution and sent me the most sincere message on 2/7/2009. It read:

> "God is forgiving and His grace has always kept me. I have to say that you truly inspired me. Honestly, I have come from a mighty long way to reach my current place. I have to pray hard constantly to steer clear of the temptation that is all around me. I have fallen short but NEVER AGAIN!!! TO GOD BE THE GLORY! Thanks for the inspiration Dr. Lindsay!
> -A true fan . . . Gareth P. Warren".

My email response to him was as follows:

> "Thanks for the kind words, Gareth. Ms Joy speaks highly of you ☺ I sent you a Facebook friend request . . . I am new to Facebook. Just joined on Tuesday . . . so, I am super pressed for new friends. LOL. Anyway . . . God bless you. It's always awesome

to see God do His thing in a young man of God. I
may give you a shout a little later. (You should come
to my Gala). Ok . . . ttyl."

Our story began with this exchange of emails and a book called,
The Best Sex of My Life: a Guide to Purity. Wow! We became friends,
and when meeting face-to-face, for the first time, I admired his
sincerity, authenticity and transparency. We developed a mental,
spiritual, and emotional intimacy that quickly allowed me to see him
as my husband. 'The list' had come to pass. I knew Gareth would be
worth the wait . . . .

Ten months and ninety-one date nights later, we were engaged
and within another ten months we were married. During the twenty
months of courtship and engagement, we set ourselves to please
God. There were moments of challenge, moments of temptation,
moments when we felt like giving in, but we held fast to our desire
to please God and not get tired of doing what was right, because we
were destined to reap (Galatians 6:9). Seriously, I liked him and he
liked me, so we had to establish boundaries to protect one another
until we got to the altar to say "I DO". At this point, I'd like to take a
moment to discuss the importance of accountability, transparency
and maturity throughout our journey.

ACCOUNTABILITY

I love and thank God for accountability. Proverbs 11:4 states, "Where
there is no counsel, the people fall; but in the multitude of counselors
there is safety." My sister Whitney called to check on me one night,
when Gareth and I were on a date. It was one of our first dates. We
were watching the movie, "Fireproof" at his house and it was well
beyond our so-called curfew. Whit, realizing the lateness of the
hour, kindly suggested that I go home. Reluctantly, I went home,
but admittedly, I needed to. I was horny and he was too. Gareth
and I already liked each other and had started to develop feelings
for one another. Boy likes girl and girl likes boy, it was natural. But,
just because I lead the Worth The Wait Revolution and have a book
about sexual purity does not make me exempt from temptation.
Actually, in some ways it made us more of a target for the enemy,
because if we messed up and fell, those who were watching our lives
would no longer have an example to follow. I thank God for Whit's
counsel and accountability, because it helped keep me on track. I

remember Minister Danielle (a big sister, friend and mentor) would ask me openly, ". . . are you two having sex or are you two kissing?" I appreciated her reaching out to me and helping me to remain accountable to her as well. Proverbs 24:6 says, "For by wise counsel you will wage your own war, and in the multitude of counselors there is safety."

The dating/courtship/engagement phase can feel like a war between your flesh, your feelings and your spirit. The strong desire to kiss, touch, hug and express intimacy is very real. I wanted to have sex . . . FOR REAL! It didn't matter that I was a virgin or a minister. I can honestly tell you that the desire to satisfy your flesh, even though you desire to honor God, is very real. At times, we hugged too tight and for too long, but we surrounded ourselves with wise people that would help us maintain a walk of purity. Sexual temptations of the past were revisited, but we overcame. We were determined to have our first kiss on our wedding day, October 30, 2010. Furthermore, we greatly anticipated our wedding night, the night I gave the gift of my virginity to my husband. Woohoo! (I will talk more on that topic a little later in the book). To accomplish the goal of sexual purity, you must remain teachable, regardless of your age or stage in life. Remember this: "A man who isolates himself seeks his own desire; he rages against all wise judgment." (Proverbs 18:1) Don't isolate yourself from your parents, Pastors, accountability partners and those who can protect you from your own emotions, desires and hormones.

Marriage Made EZ, the marriage outreach ministry of our Pastors, Drs. Mike and DeeDee Freeman, also played an instrumental role in our development and transition toward marriage. On a monthly basis, these sessions provided insight and instruction regarding the common issues challenging most marriages; money, sex, and communication. Proverbs 19:20 says, "Listen to counsel and receive instruction, that you may be wise in your latter days." Gareth and I wanted to prepare for the years ahead and surround ourselves with other couples endeavoring to do the same. We submitted to our Pastors, but we also submitted to our premarital counselors, Pastor Rick and Minister Karen Wooten. They poured thirty-seven years of experience into our premarital preparation. They corrected, challenged and encouraged us. We shared our apprehensions, reservations, challenges and weaknesses with them, and in exchange the Lord honored us. It wasn't always easy to let people in on our frustrations, failures and temptations, but Proverbs 9:8b-9 states, ". . . rebuke a wise man and he will love you. Give instruction to a wise man, and he will be wiser; teach a just man, and he will increase in learning." In my opinion, it is very dangerous to begin dating, courting and preparing for marriage without proper godly accountability, wise counsel and a heart to please God. Everyone, I repeat, EVERYONE needs the training required to be able to submit, listen and receive correction from another respected person. According to Proverbs, this process facilitates growth and learning.

TRANSPARENCY

Transparency is vital but not necessarily easy. It can be difficult to reveal and tell all. Even though my future husband read my own book that discussed many of my bad choices, there were still things for us to discuss. It was challenging talking about overcoming masturbation and childhood curiosities of "spin the bottle", "truth or dare" and "playing house", but it was essential. Being a virgin didn't make me perfect. I was coming to our relationship with a past that was covered by the blood of Jesus Christ, just like he was. Gareth had to talk to me about his past; the women, the sex, the manipulation, and the aftermath. Yet, our honesty built trust and our transparency built respect and compassion. When you are in careful consideration of a covenant companion, it is critical to be transparent about your weaknesses and your strengths. You can build a foundation, not based upon perfection or your own ability to maintain your purity, but upon the grace of God and the power of the blood of Jesus. "Except the Lord builds the house, they labor in vain who build it . . ." (Psalms 127:1 NKJV) We were determined to let the Lord build our relationship.

MATURITY

It takes real maturity to be able to maintain a courtship/engagement relationship with someone while endeavoring to maintain a totally committed love relationship with Jesus Christ. When you are growing in love with someone, I think it's very important to never leave your *first love* (Revelation 2:4). The Lord is our first love. Honestly, I had to consistently remind myself to keep first things, first. The excitement of courting, dating, talking, and preparing for intimacy, can cause your heart to shift. At times I had to remind myself not to worship the creation, but the creator. I was so excited about Gareth and our time of coming together that I had to check myself. Was I excited about going to church to hear the Word? Or, was I excited about coming to church because he was going to be there and we were going to have a date night afterwards? I had to constantly guard my heart and maintain the proper focus. I encourage you to do the same. Enjoy the journey, enjoy the relationship, but don't allow it to consume you. The Lord wants us to be happy and enjoy the process, but I think we need to be cautious about not allowing marriage (and all of its glamour) to become an idol. I certainly desired to be married and wanted Gareth to be my husband, but I had to make sure I had no other 'gods' in my life. Exodus 20:3 clearly states, "You shall have no other gods before Me." I was not going to worship the idea of marriage and make it a 'god' in my life. Unfortunately, when people are not walking in real maturity this temptation is difficult to resist. Consequently, they can be easily caught up in the excitement of the moment and not heed God's voice when He challenges them to slow down, break-up or even re-evaluate the relationship. Courtship and engagement require maturity, because there are times when it is determined that the person you are dating/courting/considering for marriage is no longer meeting the expectations or qualifications necessary to continue with the relationship. Will you obey the voice of God and walk away? Or, will you ignore the voice of God and regret the decision later? To compromise now, is to compromise for a lifetime. To ignore the voice of God in this season, will perpetuate future seasons of despair, disgust and depression. Trust me. I have been there and it's not worth it. The enemy will torment you with thoughts of discouragement and shame. During our courtship and engagement process, we really tried to allow God to speak to us independently, despite being enamored by the sparkle of marriage and a big wedding. I caution you, do not become so consumed with envisioning and planning a wedding that you neglect your first love and begin to worship the wedding day. I challenge you to walk in such maturity.

One evening after a pretty interesting drama-filled episode involving another young woman, I simply had a real, face to face conversation with Gareth. We had only known each other for a few weeks, and we were still 'friends' trying to figure out if we wanted to take our friendship down the road of courtship and exclusivity. Admittedly, Gareth had many women that were in his past, and I was well aware of them. I was cool with that, because I had a full revelation of 2 Corinthians 5:17 which states, "Therefore, if anyone is in Christ, he is a new creation; old things have passed away; behold all things have become new." He was brand new, with a clean slate as far as I was concerned. My challenge, however, was whether or not he could manage the consequences of his past relationships, such that they didn't interfere with our potentially new found relationship. That day, I recall feeling upset, confused, irritated and rather annoyed by how another young woman was disrespectful to me, in his presence. I didn't curse him out. I didn't curse her out. I didn't act a fool. I didn't get nasty. (Never let em' see you sweat!!!) As a mature woman of God, I engaged him in an honest conversation that evening. I respectfully articulated that I valued the anointing of God on my life and refused to be involved in any petty 'high-school' episodes. (Now, I know you are thinking . . . why did I have to address this issue?) I share this story, because there will be episodes where you will need to operate in honesty and maturity as well. You will need to openly communicate, be firm and unwilling to compromise on what you deserve and how you should be treated. You are worth the wait! In Gareth's defense, this episode was not his fault (it was the fault of the other young lady and her immature attitude), yet ultimately it became his responsibility. And, as a genuine man of God he took responsibility for that which was not even his fault. He "MAN-ed up"! His respect for the anointing on my life and our friendship caused him to respond with a sincere apology. He vowed to never put me in that situation again. He has since, kept that promise. We established such boundaries early on, and committed to maintain them. This requires real maturity.

It takes real maturity to be able to carefully navigate the waters of such a relationship and recognize that you have areas of your own personal life that require growth, development, and transformation. My relationship with Gareth revealed areas where I needed to work on my attitude, my love walk, my discipline and my selflessness. I had to take a careful inspection of the unsupervised areas of my life. After all, someone was about to come into the innermost parts of my life, my home, my finances, my family and my faith. Was I truly prepared for that? Are you prepared for that? Being single for 34 years created an independent, self-centered, me-driven disposition that needed to be submitted to God and reformed into an inter-dependent, Christ-centered, others-driven disposition. It takes maturity for us to allow the Holy Spirit to come into our hearts and do a work that only He can do. According to Philippians 1:6 MSG, ". . . there has never been the slightest doubt in my mind that the God Who started this great work in you would keep at it and bring it to a flourishing finish on the very day Christ Jesus appears." Spiritual maturity is a process that never ends and is necessary for successful relationships.

10 CHOICES TO KEEP *"US"* OUT OF TROUBLE

You may remember from my first book *The Best Sex of My Life: A Guide to Purity*, I discussed the '10 Choices to Keep You Out of Trouble'. I want to revisit this lesson. I had to continue to apply these principles to my life during our courtship and engagement. Just for the sake of review, I will list the ten choices below.

1) Guard your heart (Proverbs 4:20-23)

2) Honor your parents, Pastors and mentors (Ephesians 6:2-3)

3) Hang with people who have your answer and get away from people who have your problem (1 Corinthians 15:33, Proverbs 12: 26, Proverbs 13:20)

4) Pursue sexual purity (1 Thessalonians 4: 3-8)

5) Build your self-esteem around the Word of God (Psalms 139:14-16, 1 Peter 2:9)

6) Go to church, Bible study and sessions that promote your spiritual growth (Hosea 4:6, Romans 12:2)

7) Get a vision for every area of your life: your mate, your education, your profession, your future, your ministry etc . . . (Proverbs 29:18, Habakkuk 2: 2-4)

8) Pray consistently (Romans 8: 26)

9) Change your attitude (Walk in love) (1 Corinthians 13: 4-11)

10) Stop the sin (1 Corinthians 15:34, 1 John 1:9)

GUARD YOUR HEART

My son, give attention to my words; Incline your ear to my sayings.
Do not let them depart from your eyes; Keep them in the midst
of your heart; For they are life to those who find them,
And health to all their flesh. Keep your heart with all diligence,
For out of it spring the issues of life.—Proverbs 4:20-23

Chris Brown, Usher, Trey Songz, Tank, Jamie Foxx, Maxwell and Robin Thicke were artists we had to resist the temptation to listen to, even though they produced songs people would typically listen to, while being in a dating/courtship phase. Gareth and I had to guard our hearts. There were certain movies we couldn't watch and we were very selective about what music we listened to. Not that we were trying to be super-saved or super-spiritual, but we recognized that we desperately needed to remain on guard with things we were watching and listening to. Honestly, certain music caused us both to become very sexually aroused, and because we knew that, we prevented it from happening. Now, you might not even like these artists. Instead, you may like Lil Wayne, Drake, Jay-Z, Kanye West, Justin Bieber and/or Maroon 5. In my humble opinion, you really need to guard yourself from the things they discuss in their music as well. We understood that music is powerful and persuasive. It creates a charged environment and emotionally conducive atmosphere. With our mutual attraction and hormones raging, we decided to guard ourselves instead of trusting our flesh by saying, "we can handle it". Believe me! The words "I can handle it" have gotten me into more trouble than I'd like to admit. I thought I could handle watching certain things, listening to certain things and being in certain environments but 'it' ended up handling *me*. Moreover, Jesus said it like this in the Message Bible:

> "But don't think you've preserved your virtue simply by staying out of bed. Your heart can be corrupted by lust even quicker than your body. Those leering looks you think nobody notices—they also corrupt."
>
> Matthew 5:27-28

As I discussed in my first book, our eye gate and ear gate are the channels by which things can enter into our hearts and during our dating, guarding our hearts was critical to achieving our goal of sexual purity. The real question is, "will you be completely honest with yourself about how you need to guard your own heart"? Which lyrics are polluting your thought life and what images (whether from movies, videos or the Internet) are corrupting your pursuit of sexual purity? Most people are too lazy and immature to put in the real work of guarding their hearts. However, YOU are not like most people, which is why you are reading this book. YOU are ready for the challenge and ready to do the necessary work.

HONORING OUR PARENTS, PASTORS AND MENTORS

"Honor your father and mother," which is the first commandment with promise: "that it may be well with you and you may live long on the earth".—Ephesians 6:2-3

Honoring our parents, Pastors and mentors was a key element to our sexual purity walk, as a couple. When I met Gareth, I was thirty-two years old and grown! I was a practicing anesthesiologist, with my own house, my own car, my own bills, my own life; good and grown! Did I say, GROWN? Yet, because of the great respect I had for my parents and Pastors, I introduced Gareth to them very early in our relationship. Not because I needed to, but because I wanted to. Again, being a mature, successful adult, I still valued their opinions and advice.

Perhaps, if they would have deemed Gareth to be unsuitable or discerned something I couldn't see about him, we might not be together today. I know this sounds crazy to some of you, but that's how much I truly honor my parents and Pastors. Granted, no one is perfect but I recognized my parents and Pastors as a critical part of God's protection plan for my life. Pastors have been given the authority from God to watch over our souls (Hebrews 13:17). If you trust them to watch over your soul with respect to other areas of your life, why wouldn't you seek their counsel and approval concerning one of the most important decisions of your life; your covenant companion!

Usually fear, rejection, insecurity, rebellion and pride prevent us from humbling ourselves, being honest with ourselves and getting the information we need from those who can provide it candidly. They advised me to enjoy my time with Gareth, but to proceed with caution and allow Holy Spirit time to expose and reveal anything that was hidden from the natural eye. Over time, the Holy Spirit did reveal things about Gareth, but He revealed things about me as well. We both possessed areas in which we could improve individually. Inevitably, however, as our relationship matured into a courtship and engagement, they approved and accepted our relationship. I think it's worthy to mention that Gareth sought the approval of my Dad, Dr. Lonnie Marsh II as well as my Pastor, Dr. Michael A.

Freeman before even proposing to me. He respected and honored the position these men had (and continue to have) in my life. When you honor and respect such authority in your personal life, God is obligated to bless and honor your relationship.

HANG WITH PEOPLE WHO HAVE YOUR ANSWER, GET AWAY FROM PEOPLE WHO HAVE YOUR PROBLEM

He who walks with wise men will be wise, but the companion of fools will be destroyed.—Proverbs 13:20

Many of you may recall from my first book, that this statement happens to be my Pastor's motto. I have learned this principle from him. Gareth and I began to separate from our single friends, not in a bad way, but in an effort to build meaningful relationships with other Christian couples. This was for the purpose of accountability, but also for the purpose of developing, maturing and enriching our young relationship. Proverbs 27:7 states, "As iron sharpens iron, so a man sharpens the countenance of his friend." As singles, prior to knowing each other, we had already dismissed the friends participating in casual sex, intimate touching, bumping & grinding, friends with benefits, oral sex, booty calls, strip clubs, adultery, smoking weed, getting high, getting drunk, porn, and those frequenting the club scene. The Apostle Paul said it this way, "When I was a child, I spoke as a child, I understood as a child, I thought as a child; but when I became a man, I put away childish things" (1 Corinthians 13:11). My Pastor, Dr. Michael A. Freeman says that life is made up of a series of spirit-filled, spirit-led, spirit-acknowledged decisions. We decided that those things were no longer going to be a part of our lifestyle prior to meeting one another, nor could we closely associate with those who participated in them. Timothy wrote:

> Flee also youthful lust; but pursue righteousness, faith, love, peace with those who call upon the name of the Lord with a pure heart.
>
> 2 Timothy 2:22 (NKJV)

The same verse in the Message Bible translation reads:

> Run away from infantile indulgence. Run after
> mature righteousness—faith, love, peace—joining
> those who are in honest and serious prayer before
> God.
>
> 2 Timothy 2:22 (MSG)

We made a spirit-led decision to run away from 'the wrong' and run toward 'the right'. I heard this analogy that's simple but it makes complete sense. The analogy goes like this, "friends are like elevators, they either take you 'up' or 'down' ". I suggest that you take an inventory of your current relationships, determining to cultivate the ones that are pulling you up higher, elevating you to the next level and discontinuing the ones that are pulling you down and causing you to compromise your integrity and relationship with God.

At the time, I remember going out one night to hang with a few 'friends', when Gareth and I were in the beginning stages of courting. Everyone was pretty cordial, but one young lady in particular stood out to me that evening. When she saw Gareth, she came up to him, put her arms around his neck and hugged him very closely. Honestly, she hugged him WAY TO TIGHT!! To be really honest, she put all of her chest, breasts, and bosom on MY MAN! Really?! I couldn't believe that she thought this behavior was even appropriate. However, when I considered the environment and the people, I recognized that we had a decision to make. To remain in that environment would have been detrimental to our destiny. No one in that environment had a healthy respect for godly dating, courtship or sexual purity. In this instance, we had to make a hard decision, to walk away from certain people, places and set boundaries. You will have some tough decisions to make as well, but His grace will be sufficient, if you really desire to please Him.

PURSUE SEXUAL PURITY

For this is the will of God, your sanctification: that you should
abstain from sexual immorality; that each of you should know
how to possess his own vessel in sanctification and honor, not in
passion of lust, like the Gentiles who do not know God;
that no one should take advantage of and defraud his brother
in this matter, because the Lord is the avenger of all such,
as we also forewarned you and testified. For God did not call us to

uncleanness, but in holiness. Therefore he who rejects this
does not reject man, but God, who has also given us
His Holy Spirit.—1Thessalonians 4:3-8

Oooweee! This was hard at times; really hard. Once we had become more intimate, emotionally, intellectually and spiritually, the physical intimacy wanted to naturally follow suit, especially after the engagement. However, we had to constantly manage those emotions, hormones, passions and desires. We had to be brutally honest with one another. If his cologne was turning me on to the point where my flesh was going to get out of control, I would tell him. If my dress was too short or my shirt was too tight for him to handle, he would let me know. Obviously, we were deeply attracted to one another but when those hugs became too tight and too long, we had to be honest with one another.

God has given us a sex 'drive', not a sex 'walk' or a sex 'crawl'. In other words, like a car, your body can go from 0 to 60 miles per hour in 2.9 seconds like the *Ferrari F50 GT1 4.7l V12* or faster. As women, our bodies begin to secrete a natural lubricant that prepares the vagina for the entrance of the penis. Male arousal is a little more obvious as demonstrated by the erect penis. At this stage in our relationship, we would hug, hold hands, and exhibit closeness but we would carefully watch crossing that fine line into foreplay. Foreplay, as defined by Merriam-Webster, is erotic stimulation preceding sexual intercourse. In other words, foreplay by design and definition is an appetizer or teaser, leading up to the main course. In proper dining etiquette, it is not considered wise to become full off of the appetizers, because the main course is suppose to be the highlight of the meal. Unfortunately, many young Christian are devouring the foreplay appetizers. Gareth and I didn't want that to be our testimony, so we pressed through those moments and often had to 'flee', just as Paul instructed the Corinthian church:

> Flee sexual immorality. Every sin that a man does
> is outside the body, but he who commits sexual
> immorality sins against his own body.
> 1 Corinthians 6:18

That meant one of us had to say: "Goodbye, see ya later, I'll holler, Adios, Peace out, Deuces, Farewell, Au revoir, Gone, I'm outty!!!!!" One of us had to be the mature one that made the decision to 'flee'. Real talk! I wish I could tell you that this is an easy process and when you decide to 'flee', angels will arrive to personally escort you home on a 'floating cloud of glory'. But, the reality is that you will have to remember the difference between love and lust. Furthermore, you will have to remember the high price that was paid for you, (the shed blood of Jesus Christ). If you understand that great price you will run before giving out discounts. No discounts while dating, no discounts while courting and no discounts while engaged. Here is the age old question, "Why should you buy the cow, if you can get the milk for free?" Answer: There is no reason, no incentive, no need to buy the cow. If the cow continues to supply free milk, the milk's value and the cow's value are greatly reduced and free milk will keep that cow feeling empty, misused and unwanted. This is the harsh reality of giving out discounts. Of course, we are not cows, but rather sons and daughters of the Most High God, so let's be mindful not to discount the price that was paid for us on Calvary.

I wrote the following article for *Essence Magazine* in 2009 while dating Gareth. The article was never published due to some administrative and editorial changes. However, I wanted to share the article with you, because it reflects the sexual purity mindset I wanted to convey to the *Essence* readers, as well as my own readers. The article reads as follows:

So, I am a virgin. And yes, virgins do still exist. I am an attractive, 33 year old virgin. But, I'm quite normal . . . I went to medical school, I like BCBG, I pledged Delta Sigma Theta in undergrad, but I made a decision to wait to have sex, within marriage. Some people think this is absurd, and other people applaud me. Either way, HIV, STDs or an unwanted pregnancy is never a concern of mine, but my reasons for abstaining run much deeper. The temptation and desire to have sex is just as real for a virgin as it is for anyone else, yet I have a few personal guidelines that I use to help maintain my decision.

1) I don't date guys who do not honor my decision to abstain until marriage.

This does not mean that I only date male virgins. I have met plenty of intelligent, attractive, ambitious, God-fearing men that understand abstinence and have recommitted to this lifestyle, after being very sexually active. The man I am currently dating is a phenomenal man, who respects, admires, and loves me, and in spite of his own sexual past, and he is currently living an abstinent life (which he embarked upon prior to us meeting). Our relationship flows quite well and we

17

have been dating for almost a year. He is an amazing man, and we are seriously contemplating marriage. I am fully aware of his past relationships, but we do not allow the past to dictate our future. In the meantime, we do not spend time in each other's bedrooms (to avoid the temptation), and we have other married couples that we are accountable to, in our relationship. They help us to stay focused during this season of our relationship. At one time I was interested in a man, who didn't quite understand the importance of applying the abstinence message to his daily life and despite what I perceived to be a mutual attraction, our interaction did not grow beyond a professional friendship. In the beginning, I was disappointed, but soon realized that we were not a good fit on so many levels.

2) I am open and honest about being a virgin.

"Hi, I'm Lindsay and I'm a virgin,". . . . is not the first thing that comes out of my mouth, but it's not something that I am ashamed of or embarrassed about, so it will be discussed relatively early in the relationship. People tend to put on masks, especially during the beginning stages of a relationship, when honesty and transparency is really needed. I think my honesty and transparency has helped me to avoid wasting time within relationships that did not have a future. I think it's a good thing to be clear about your boundaries. One man, I dated in undergrad challenged my boundaries, and I found myself kissing, touching, and heavy petting etc . . . , which was uncomfortable for me. I had to step back, and break off that relationship, recognizing that it was causing me to compromise on my core values. We started off with the same desire to remain abstinent, but slowly got off course. We never had sex, but we came close to it. Other men that I have seriously dated in the past truly respected my guidelines and boundaries. Even though our relationships did not progress, I never found myself regretting 'something' I'd done within the relationship. Why? I never compromised who I was, to be within the relationship. I did not allow my emotions to supersede my decision to remain abstinent.

Ladies, I think that any respectful man who is worthy of your affection and love will be willing to wait and pay the price for you. It is an honorable thing for a man to understand your value and pursue you. In this dating process, it is ok to be honest and transparent. It will prevent dead-end relationships, in the long run. My decision has been to wait until marriage, and I encourage any

*other woman who decides to wait, as well. In spite of your past or
past relationships, please understand that it is never too late
to be WORTH THE WAIT!!*
Lindsay Marsh, MD (Written September 2009)

BUILD YOURSELF ESTEEM AROUND
THE WORD OF GOD

*But you are a chosen generation, a royal priesthood,
a holy nation, His own special people, that you may proclaim
the praises of Him who called you out of darkness into His
marvelous light.—1 Peter 2:9*

I'm thankful that Gareth and I were well aware of our identity in
Christ Jesus while courting, and that our self-esteem was/is rooted in
Him. Unfortunately, many people are experiencing an identity crisis.
Young men and women have no clue that their identity, self-worth,
self-value and self-esteem that should be based upon the Word of
God. Instead they use external things to define themselves; including
money, cars, professions, degrees, titles, associations, prosperity
decoys, girlfriends, boyfriends, and/or organizations. You have to be
honest with yourself. Does your girlfriend or boyfriend define you?
Is your self-esteem tied to his or her existence? Does 'smashing'
(having cheap sex with) all the girls you can provide a sense of
worth and value? I am amazed by the young women that think
they are pretty and use their beauty to manipulate others. I am
equally amazed by the young men that think they are God's gift to
the female population; self-absorbed, immature, preoccupied with
their own external validation system. Don't get me wrong. There
is nothing wrong with being confident, but there is a difference
between confidence, cockiness and complete foolishness.

Gareth is a handsome Johns Hopkins Carey Business School
MBA graduate, valued financial professional within a prestigious
public institution, and a reputable community leader, serving as an
Advisory Board Member for the Morgan State University Graves
Honors Program. Nevertheless, none of these things replaced or
were substitutes for his self-esteem being rooted in the Word of
God. I am an attractive anesthesiologist, author, minister and leader.
Nevertheless, none of these things replace or were substitutes for
what the Word says about me. 1 Peter 2:9 and Colossians 2: 9-10 state
respectively, ". . . you are a chosen generation, a royal priesthood, a

holy nation, His own special people . . ." and ". . . you are complete in Him". The titles and the 'stuff' do not make me! I am complete in Him! Furthermore, when I was single I recognized that a 'boyfriend' or a future 'husband' did not define me. My self-esteem was/is built around the Word of God, not around my social status, Facebook status, Twitter following or Instagram pictures with my boo!!

Do not be deceived, folks! We must build our self-esteem on the unchangeable foundation of God's Word. Don't get caught up in relationships because of their popularity, provision or prominence. You may look cute together, people may celebrate your relationship or you might receive a lot of gifts and perks, but don't let these things distract you from keeping God first and maintaining your boundaries.

GO TO CHURCH, BIBLE STUDY AND SESSIONS THAT PROMOTE YOUR SPIRITUAL GROWTH

My people are destroyed for lack of knowledge.
Because you have rejected knowledge, I also will reject you
from being priest for Me; because you have forgotten the law
of your God, I also will forget your children.—Hosea 4:6

You can't stop attending church once you start dating and courting. You can't stop coming, participating and serving once you establish a connection with someone. A distraction, by definition, is that which distracts, divides the attention or prevents concentration, according to Dictionary.com. Unfortunately, the new found relationships in our lives can become 'distractions', dividing our attention and concentration from the things that were once important. Paul warns us of this:

> But I want you to be without care. He who is unmarried cares for the things of the Lord, how he may please the Lord. But he who is married cares about the things of the world, how he may please his wife. There is a difference between a wife and a virgin. The unmarried woman cares about the things of the Lord, that she may be holy both in body and in spirit. But she who is married cares about the things of the world, how she may please her husband. And this I say for your own profit, not that

> I may put a leash on you, but for what is proper and
> that you may serve the Lord without *distraction*.
>
> 1 Corinthians 7:32-35

In other words, do not allow someone who is not (currently) your husband or wife to break your concentration and divide your attention from the things in life that really matter. Growing in the Lord, serving Him, developing your destiny, and walking out your purpose are areas in which you cannot afford distractions. If you stop coming to church, Bible study and those empowerment sessions He has ordained for your life, you will be forced to rely, trust and lean on your own understanding. Proverbs 3:5-6 warns against this kind of self-reliance saying, "Trust in the Lord with all your heart, and *lean not on your own understanding*; in all your ways acknowledge Him, and He shall direct your path". Gareth and I continued to make church, bible study and serving a top priority because we did not want to become a distraction to one another; a burden instead of a blessing. It's imperative that you remain steadfast and immovable, always abounding in the work of the Lord, knowing that your labor is not in vain in the Lord regardless of your single, dating, waiting or courting 'status'(1 Corinthians 15:58)!

GET A VISION FOR EVERY AREA OF YOUR LIFE

> *Where there is no vision, the people cast off restraint;*
> *but he that keepeth the law, happy is he.—Proverbs 29:18 (ASV)*

Can you see yourself doing something bigger and something better than what you are experiencing today? I encourage you to write a vision for every area of your life. Dream big! Supersize your goals! God is the One that causes our dreams and visions to come true. Academically, professionally, spiritually, financially, socially and within our families, He is able to do exceedingly, abundantly above all that we can ask or think (Ephesians 3:20)! As early as my preteen years, I had a vision for my husband. I stapled that childhood vision to my newly revised young adult vision, and continued to add to it, as the Holy Spirit guided me.

My 7th grade vision for my husband consisted of the following:

"The Perfect Man":

- Intelligent
- An athlete's body
- Humorous-serious
- Persistent (able to accept no and come back for more)???
- Delicious face: lips, eyes, eyebrows, handsome
- Classy
- A guy all other girls want, but he's dedicated to me
- Charismatic
- Relaxed
- Outspoken
- Reliable
- "A man of his word"
- Diligent
- Somewhat overprotective (so that I know he cares), but not overbearing
- He prioritizes
- Respects me
- Sensitive
- Trustworthy
- Responsible
- Courteous
- Well-groomed
- Understanding
- Innovative
- Sexy
- A good conversationist (I made up my own word ☺)
- A good friend
- Unselfish
- Giving
- Dedicated

(This is a pretty good list for a girl who grew up in a Presbyterian church and didn't really have a real relationship with the Lord.)

It's fun for me to reflect back on this childhood vision and the more mature version composed years later, because it helps me to remember and appreciate the faithfulness of God. Anyone that knows or has met Gareth knows that He meets all of these qualifications. When God says in Habakkuk 2: 2, "write the vision and make it plain", that is exactly what He means. The Message Bible says:

> Write this. Write what you see. Write it out in big
> block letters so that it can be read on the run. This

vision-message is a witness pointing to what's coming. It aches for the coming—it can hardly wait! And, it doesn't lie. If it seems slow in coming, wait. It's on the way. It will come right on time.

Habakkuk 2:2-3

God is sooooooo faithful! Gareth came into my life when I was 32. Right on time! Although, it didn't always feel like it was 'right on time'. At The George Washington University, I completed undergraduate, medical school and my anesthesia residency according to an academic/professional vision that I had since I was a little girl. It was my dream to grow up and become a doctor. Additionally, I had completed my first book, which was a secret vision of mine to capture the memoirs of why I wanted to keep my virginity until marriage. I was serving and enjoying the maturation of the young men and women who were a part of our college outreach, "WordUp". Then . . . Gareth showed up. Why hadn't the Lord brought him into my life earlier? Perhaps, he would've distracted me from my studies or maybe I would not have been motivated to write my book. It's probable that I would've missed valuable time with God that was essential to my destiny, compelling me to move forward with the 'I AM WORTH THE WAIT' shirts and the Worth The Wait Revolution. Psalm 31:15a states, "My times are in Your hands." As I reflect back and marvel at how strategically calculated this journey has been from me moving to DC when I was 18, to connecting with my Pastors and church, to being exempt from taking the MCAT, to writing *The Best Sex of My Life: a guide to Purity*, it has been the manifestation of one vision (dream) after the other. Vision-casting and dream-casting for every area of your life, will discipline and restrain you. Proverbs 29:18a states, "Where there is no revelation (vision), the people cast off restraint". I am thankful for the visions and dreams I had as a single woman, because they restrained me from the temptation to settle for 'a mediocre man' (unworthy of my love, my time and my anointing) and 'a mediocre life'.

Now, for the sake of self-examination, I have a few questions for you, regarding the vision that you have for your future mate.

- Why are you compromising?
- Why are you tolerating raggedy relationships?
- Why do you compromise on the 'non-negotiables'? (You date unsaved, unchurched, undisciplined people)

- Why do you settle for 'projects' or people that require fix-ups?
- Why not let patience do the work for you (James 1:4)?

Let me remind you that God loves you and you don't have to compromise on the important, non-negotiable matters of your relationships. Don't become desperate, but rather become devoted to God's vision for your future.

PRAY CONSISTENTLY

Pray without ceasing.—1 Thessalonians 5:17

I dated a few other guys before dating my husband. I'll admit that I was selective, but I did have a few friendships prior to meeting Gareth. In most of these relationships I relied heavily on my prayer life, communication with the Father and the peace of God to determine if I should continue to talk on the phone, hang out, or even entertain relationships. You should be talking to the Father and He should be talking to you. More importantly, you should be listening. Continue to listen to God, your Pastor, your parents and other voices of godly authority in your life. God can and will speak through them on your behalf, as well. He will also lead you by His peace. Colossians 3:15a says, "And let the peace of God rule in your hearts, to which also you were called in one body". I use the peace of God to decide and govern the affairs of my life. When my relationship with Gareth was brand new, I had peace and I used that same peace as a guide throughout our relationship to decide whether or not to proceed. God has promised to lead and guide us into all truth and I think part of that leading and guiding comes from a direct sensing of His peace and His presence in our lives. I have never heard God speak to me in an audible voice, but I have had Him to lead me by His peace. When you are in constant communication with Him, He will make your path clear and straight (Proverbs 3:5-6). Unfortunately, one time I ignored the lack of peace I had regarding a certain guy. Yes, I ignored God. Perhaps it was because this guy was a really cute Christian leader, quite charismatic, and someone that was being pursued by many other young ladies. Well, unfortunately, I ignored the voice of God and casually proceeded with the relationship. Regrettably, I opened the door to two years of unnecessary drama and disobedience. For what? It wasn't worth it. Trust me. Do not be lead by your emotions or hormones, but allow God to guide you by His peace, through constant communication with Him.

After Gareth and I completed our premarital counseling, the Lord led me to write a personal prayer for our marriage. We were embarking on the journey of a lifetime, and we needed to continually acknowledge God throughout the journey. I consistently pray this prayer over our relationship. I encourage you to create and customize your own prayer for godly marriage you aspire to have one day.

Prayer for Gareth and Lindsay Warren

Father, I bless and honor You. There is nothing too impossible or too hard for You. I thank You for our relationship and our marriage. I decree our latter end shall be greater than our former, and the love we have now will continue to grow, develop and increase even beyond our marriage. We are best friends. We love each other at all times. As iron sharpens iron, we sharpen one another's countenance. We lay down our life for one another. We enjoy each other's company. I thank You for turning our hearts toward one another. We are face to face with you and one another. Gareth has made a covenant with his eyes and does not look upon another woman, lustfully. I have made a covenant with my eyes and I do not look upon another man, lustfully. He is a faithful man and abounds in blessings. He is a man of integrity, character and excellence. His children are blessed after him. He is a good man and leaves an inheritance for his children's children. He is a man after God's own heart and he loves me as Christ loves the church. He dwells with me according to knowledge and I honor, respect and appreciate him as the head of own home. He is the prophet, priest and king our family. I am a virtuous woman and my price is far above rubies. The heart of my husband, Gareth P. Warren can safely trust in me, even as I trust him. Strength and honor are my clothing and on my tongue is the law of kindness, and I do not eat the bread of idleness. My children call me blessed as Gareth does also . . . and he praises me. Many daughters have done well, but I excel them all. Gareth and I submit to one another. I submit to Gareth, as submitting to Christ. We are both quick to hear, slow to speak, slow to wrath. We are both quick to forgive. All old things in other relationships have passed away, and now all things have become new in Christ Jesus. The anointing of God on our relationship removes burdens, every generational curse, every hurt, and destroys every yoke . . . every ungodly soul tie. Our souls are fully restored, in Jesus name. We walk in love. Gareth and I are patient, kind, not easily angered, take no record of a wrong done, we endure all things, hope all things, believe all things. Our love never fails. Gareth and I's marriage bed is blessed and undefiled. It is the Garden of Eden, the garden of delight. I am the loving doe that satisfies Gareth all the days of his life. He drinks waters from his own cistern. We render unto one another due benevolence. To one another, we are fairer than 10,000. We are friends, but more importantly, lovers. We like each other. We are happy. I decree the spirit of love, joy, peace, and happiness reign in our relationship. I decree that Gareth and I walk in the unity of the Spirit, the unity of the faith, and are in agreement with the Spirit of God and the Word of God. What Satan intended for evil, God is turning around for His good and for His glory. The best is yet to come. The perfect will of God is surely coming to pass in this union, in Jesus' name. All things are working together for OUR good because we love You, God and we are called according to Your purpose and plan. Our eyes are seeing it, our ears are hearing it, and our hearts are receiving . . . the things God prepared beforehand for us . . . . and Father, You are revealing it to us by Your Spirit. We receive it all. I am my beloved's and he is mine . . . his banner over me is love. I have ravished his heart, as his friend and spouse. We are living out a modern day Song of Solomon . . . . and Father God, You are causing our dreams to come true! In Jesus' Name. Amen!

CHANGE YOUR ATTITUDE

Love suffers long and is kind; love does not envy; love does not parade itself, is not puffed up; does not behave rudely, does not seek its own, is not provoked, thinks no evil; 6does not rejoice in iniquity, but rejoices in the truth; bears all things, believes all things, hopes all things, endures all things. Love never fails. But whether there are prophecies, they will fail; whether there are tongues, they will cease; whether there is knowledge, it will vanish away. For we know in part and we prophesy in part, but when that which is perfect has come, then that which is in part will be done away. When I was a child, I spoke as a child, I understood as a child, I thought as a child; but when I became a man, I put away childish things.
—1 Corinthians 13: 4-11

I could write two more books about my attitude, alone. Wow, how I've grown! I have matured from the single, self-centered, prideful, 'it's all about me' mindset. Marriage is about compromise, teamwork, sacrifice, humility, submission, surrender, partnership, camaraderie, and compassion. I'm not perfect. I have not yet arrived, but I have come a long way. Especially when 1 Corinthians 13 talks about not keeping score, not taking a record of wrong-doing and not being easily angered. It was time to put away childish things. These were areas that I definitely needed to work on. I didn't want to bring that kind of attitude into my marriage. Purposing in my heart to be patient and kind, even when I felt like being impatient and nasty, was the real groundwork I had to do within my heart. Courtship began to expose those inadequacies and inconsistencies in my character. The Holy Spirit challenged me with these questions and now I challenge you.

<u>Would YOU want to date YOU? Would YOU want to marry YOU?</u>

- Financially? (Are you in serious debt? Do you know how to save? Are you a tither?)
- Spiritually? (Do you pray? Are you consistent? Can you withstand the weight of marriage?)
- Intellectually? (Are you a critical-thinker? Are you intellectually-stimulating?)
- Emotionally? (Are you stable? Are you bipolar? Are you controlled by your feelings?)
- Physically? (Are you happy with your body? Do you have a healthy body image?)
- Attitude? (Are you easy-going or hard to deal with? Are you a 'piece of work'?

Often times we believe God for 'the best', but we don't want to put in the work TO BE THE BEST. As a single, I recognized that my future husband deserved the best! Well, that meant I had some growing up to do. That meant I had some work to do. My attitude surrounding so many areas began to change. I developed a debt-free mentality and paid off everything attached to me, except my mortgage debt payoff (coming soon). I began to dig deeper and make the necessary adjustments in my private life, so that my private and public life would be in alignment. I began to eat better, think smarter, spend wiser, and 'get a grip' on out of control areas. I was taking myself too seriously at times and furthermore, the world did not revolve around me!! (I'm airing my dirty laundry so that you can ask yourself the hard questions, be honest with yourself and get to work on YOU!)

STOP THE SIN

Awake to righteousness, and do not sin . . .—1 Corinthians 15:34a

When I had challenges with masturbation, I ultimately had to be the one to make the decision to stop. While in high school and involved with my first real boyfriend, I had to be the one to actually decide to stop the humping, rubbing and touching. The power to stop lies within *your own will*. The power to stop is *your own decision*. The power to stop is closer than you think. I love how the Word of God takes away all of our excuses. The Apostle Paul wrote:

> I have strength for all things in Christ who empowers me, I am ready for anything and equal to anything through Him Who infuses strength into me; I am self-sufficient in Christ sufficiency.
>
> Philippians 4:13 (AMP)

Marriage doesn't cure a spirit of lust. Marriage is not the answer to unresolved and uncontrolled flesh issues. Marriage will not address the root of the problem that is causing the sin. Gareth and I were mature enough to put a stop to any sin issues that were brought to our attention during our dating/courtship/engagement process. It takes maturity, discipline and a genuine love for God to stop behaviors and attitudes that do not please Him. Jesus said, ". . . If you love Me, keep My commandments" (John 14:15). It was my love for Jesus that gave me the desire to change. In turn, it was His great love for me that persuaded me to change, in spite of my stubbornness.

I ask you . . . do you really love Jesus? How well are you keeping His commandments? I encourage you to love Him through your obedience, not just your lip service and mere church attendance. Men and women alike, let's show Him how much we love Him, by keeping His commandments and putting a stop to the masturbation, oral sex, porn, shacking, sneaking and all sexual perversions of the past and present. Stop it, because you love Him. His grace will be sufficient for you!

With God's grace, Gareth and I applied the "10 Choices" and experienced a successful courtship and engagement. Furthermore, on October 30, 2010, God honored us because we honored Him. Our beautiful wedding and reception was featured in *The Washington Post*.   (http://www.washingtonpost.com/wp-dyn/content/

article/2010/11/11/AR2010111108576.html) God's supernatural favor was upon us every step of the way. People from all over the nation signed our wedding guest book, leaving wonderful words of encouragement and blessing.

"Any and everybody who is in Christ and "waiting" should look no further for encouragement!!! This is what happens when you do it God's way!!! Thank you both for being perfect examples to all of us, who are waiting for that blessing from God to enter our lives. Congratulations to you both and may God bless both of you for many years to come!!! And Gareth . . . thank you for being there for me in my time of need. You are truly a man of God and I am blessed to have you as a brother in Christ."

"I found out about Worth The Wait Revolution when I googled purity a few years back. I was so excited and inspired. I wondered. Did she get married? I was happy to know, tonight. Congrats, to both of you!!! I am 25. A virgin who knows I am worth the wait. I am happy I am not the only girl who decided that my first real kiss would be at the altar! No discounts . . . LOL. God richly bless you both! We are the chosen generation and sexual purity is cool! Love you. I am so happy for you both."

"Beautiful. Congratulations to the both of you and thanks for being a true example."

"You have a beautiful love story that brought tears of joy to my eyes. God is amazing. May you be blessed in your marriage forever."

"Congratulations Dr. Lindsay!!!! I have a smile from ear to ear seeing how God has made your dream come true. I've never met you in person, but I joined the Revolution almost 3 years ago. And it's been almost 3 years of celibacy for me (3 yrs!!!), largely due to God bringing your amazing ministry across my path :-) I pray many, many blessings for you both!!!!!"

"Congratulations Dr. Linds and Gareth! You have impacted my life so much! Every time a thought evens comes to my mind for me to settle or compromise, I think about your relationship and how God will give you the desires of your heart if you are obedient and patient. Thank you for being great examples! Love you both!"

*"Greetings From Nashville!! You guys are such an inspiration!!
Thank you for TRUSTING GOD enough to stay the course.
Reading your sacrifices and seeing your reward encourages
me to not get weary in well doing! I pray your marriage is
BLESSED and you continue to be AWESOME examples of GOD's
original intent for marriage and family among our culture!"*

To God be all the glory!! Yes, dreams do come true and God had exceeded all of my expectations. Just as He was faithful to me, He will be faithful to you. (Join me in a few chapters as I discuss our new, amazing 'sex life' as a newlywed couple in the chapter entitled, *The Best Sex of My Life*.)

Preface To The Confessions of A Sexual Purity Revolution

What is your confession? What is your story? What is your testimony? My prayer is that this book has been placed into your hands before the perversion of the world has an opportunity to steal, kill and destroy your future and that the pages of this book can speak louder than the sexploitation you are receiving through hip-hop, social media, entertainment, internet and the like. I hope I can minister to you before you receive ungodly counsel from your friends in the locker room, your family members at the family reunion and your friends at school. Prayerfully, this book gets into your hands before you get 'turned out' in college or swept away by a fraternity or sorority with its empty promises of popularity and fulfillment. (I am a member of Delta Sigma Theta Sorority, so don't think I'm speaking as a novice or one who is unaware of the particulars.) My desire is that this book crosses your path before the deception of this generation blinds you from the wisdom and discernment of making healthy and intelligent decisions. My Pastor, Dr. Michael A. Freeman says, "Generational curses have been broken, yet there are still generational choices to be made." We desperately need wisdom, knowledge, understanding, discernment and the Holy Spirit to make good generational choices. This book will help YOU to make proper godly generational choices.

A common saying suggests that 'experience is the best teacher'. It is *a teacher*, but it is not the *best teacher*. Clearly, *experience* has killed some people. *Experience* has resulted in some young women becoming pregnant. *Experience* has given some an incurable sexually transmitted disease, while experience has caused others to commit suicide. *Experience* has caused some to lose their gender identity, yield to sexual experimentation and confusion. Merriam-Webster defines experience as, "direct observation of or participation in events as a basis of knowledge; the fact or state of having been affected by or gained knowledge through direct observation or participation". *Experience* is NOT the best teacher. God does not want you to have direct participation or direct observation in pornography, homosexuality, abuse, molestation, promiscuity, disease, abortion, rape or experimentation. Fortunately and unfortunately, this book contains a wealth of 'experiences'. However, they are the experiences of those who are willing to share their personal setbacks, wrong turns, and poor choices, as well as their triumphs, healing and restoration. Learn from our experiences. Glean from our stories. Understand that you can overcome any situation, any setback, any disappointment, any emotional bondage, and any demonic stronghold. I am thankful to be free from masturbation and free from the poor choices of my own past. I am thankful to be free enough to boldly share my own stories with you and others across the world. I commend those who have partnered with me, by submitting their stories (confessions) to this body of work. It is a true blessing for us to come together to display the complete picture of God's grace, goodness and mercy, as each of us has our own amazing story to tell.

Matthew 2:13 describes a situation surrounding the early moments of Jesus' life and how an angel appeared to Joseph in a dream, saying, "Arise, take the young Child and His mother, flee to Egypt, and stay there until I bring you word; for Herod will seek the young Child to destroy Him". Herod, symbolically being used of Satan, was seeking to kill the Baby Jesus, who was a threat to King Herod; He was prophesied to be the 'King of the Jews'. Similarly, in Exodus 1:15-2:10, Pharaoh attempted to kill Moses and other Hebrew male children. To draw a striking parallel, I believe that Satan attempts to steal, kill and destroy in our lives when we are young, immature and vulnerable. As children, preteens and adolescents he has tried to manipulate, pervert and attack our innocence and our ignorance. It is obvious that the youth and young adults of this generation are being challenged like never before with homosexuality, sex trafficking, teen pregnancy, abortion, STDs, HIV, suicide, drug abuse, violence and bullying. Just as he tried to murder Jesus and Moses as very young children, I believe he attempts to derail and destroy our destiny as young people, as well. Satan attempts to stunt our greatness through our associations, exposures and environments, but just as Jesus and Moses escaped and fulfilled their God-ordained purpose for their generation, so will you and I!! Our destinies cannot be denied, in spite of any past situation because ALL THINGS work together for good to those who love God, to those who are called according to His purpose (Romans 8:28). We win!!

I have grown to understand more and more that ". . . we are all like an unclean thing, and all our righteousness are like filthy rags" (Isaiah 64:6). We cannot *earn* God's approval. We cannot do enough 'good works' to *earn* his favor. Our *own* 'so-called righteousness' is nothing in His sight, regardless of who we are. From the virgin to the promiscuous one, we all need the blood of Jesus to purge, cleanse and renew our conscience of dead works to serve the Living God (Hebrews 9:14). This righteousness given to us through and by the precious blood of Jesus Christ is a free gift; nothing earned or deserved. I'm thankful for the blood of Jesus which empowers us to share our testimonies without guilt and shame or condemnation. We are free, indeed, and we are grateful that God can turn our scars into stars! God can give us *beauty* for ashes (the mistakes, the hurts and the heartaches), and double honor instead of shame (Isaiah 61:3-7). As you read *The Confessions of a Sexual Purity Revolution* be blessed, be empowered and be transformed.

Gareth's Confession

Confession: By Gareth P. Warren

". . . they say experience is the best teacher, that's what they teach us in school. I say experience is the teacher of fools, because a wise man will learn from another man's errors and apply to determine what he should choose."—Da Truth

I'm about to reveal a lot of my past to you, to unveil the game for ladies and to encourage the guys to avoid the path that I took. As a young man "sexual freedom" was a more familiar phrase than "sexual purity". As a matter of fact, I had never heard the phrase "sexual purity"; nor did I know what it meant. Dating back as far as middle school, when I experimented with trying on my first condom, I have always been curious about sex. I would later discover that this was the result of generational curiosities embedded in my DNA. Growing up without the presence of my father presented a challenge in my development as a young man. Although I had many male examples in my family, there were certain lessons they were not equipped to teach me. I was never taught about sexual purity or God's desired purpose for sex.

As a child, I wasn't as exposed to sexually explicit propaganda as most youth are via media outlets and the Internet. However, this didn't diminish my desire to be sexually active. While in elementary school, I remember daringly passing notes to girls asking them to circle "yes" or "no" to be my girlfriend. Once they said yes, I remember discretely holding hands and touching their private places while watching educational movies in the library with my class. This was the beginning of a journey down a slippery slope that continued well into my adult life. As I progressed through elementary and middle school, I gained weight and became less attractive to girls.

This made it difficult to continue satisfying my sexual curiosity via touching and rubbing. The transition to middle school was difficult and impacted several areas, including my grades and self-esteem.

In an effort to fill the void and find validation, I began hanging out with an older crowd after school. On very rare occasions I experimented with alcohol and cigarettes in elementary school. As I began to hang with my new clique of friends, I used alcohol and cigarettes more frequently and eventually tried marijuana. We were all a part of a local gang called "Loop 850"; significant for the street we all grew up on. I appeared to look the same age as most of them, so when they went to clubs I was also able to get in as a result. My association with a gang seemingly helped to rebuild my confidence, but for the wrong reasons. I began to play football for my school in the 7th grade, played for the high school band drum line in the 8th grade and eventually began to lose weight, which contributed to my popularity rebound. I was later sought after to accompany an upper-class young lady to the junior/senior prom where I had a sexual encounter with her. The slippery slope I mentioned earlier got more and more slippery as I began to take advantage of my popularity rebound and the weaknesses of women.

In high school, I was a confident, likable leader. I was voted "most likely to succeed" and even "Mr. Arp High School" my senior year. I was the first and last student to win the office of student class president and the senior class president within the same year. My athletic career also proved successful in my high school years as I was sought after by many colleges at one point.

Outside of school I was a hardworking entrepreneur. My grandfather, a well-known farmer and paint & body shop owner, taught me the importance of working hard, by example. I was frequently seen with my grandfather and was eventually invited to assist him and my uncle in their paint & body shop. I was exposed to all aspects of running this business including the processes, business connections and even secrets of the trade. The training they provided made me a stickler for detail and I later became the car detail specialist. I not only made sure all cars were the cleanest they had ever been, but I developed relationships with the owners and began to detail their vehicles on a regular. While most of my friends were going to the mall, watching television or playing video games on Saturdays, I was managing my own business of detailing vehicles. This helped me to purchase my first vehicle and finance my drinking, smoking and clubbing habits. While in high school I moved out of my mom's house to house-sit for my uncle on a long-term basis. I left my mom and younger siblings behind. My decision to make this move was against my mom's will and premature. I had access to several guns, alcohol, marijuana and other inappropriate things. Hindsight is 20/20 and foresight is the will of God, so take note if you are even close to making such irrational moves. My friends and I often used these weapons when going to clubs and to burglarize vehicles. Very few people from my community were aware that I was involved in such acts, which allowed me to continue them.

Many of you are wondering why I am providing background that doesn't seem to discuss my sexual purity testimony. Well, it really is connected and this is why. As a well-known student, active musician at my church, star athlete, and young entrepreneur, I led a double life. Many saw me as a respectable young man in my local community. They had no idea that I was drinking, smoking, engaging in criminal activity at clubs or even connected to various illegal activities. I am not proud of my behavior, but it was the result of a lack of discipline. My money, my leadership roles and my older friends made me feel untouchable. I believed I could have whatever I desired. I believed I could have sex with any woman I wanted. Make no mistake, I was not and have never been a rapist. Instead, I had a natural ability that gave me confidence to get women. Women are drawn to men of power and confidence.

The lack of authority and accountability in my life opened the door to even more pre-marital sex. I was taught that "numbers" mattered when it came to having sex. This was a cultural norm, not just evident among the males in my family but also with other males I associated with. I began developing "soul-ties" during this time as well. I often listened to my uncles and other males say things like, "I hit that" or "I'll tap that" or "Would you cut her"? ("Cut" is slang indicating sexual intercourse). They were huge flirts and often recklessly confident in their ability to convince women to have sex with them and others. After analyzing the movie "Waiting to Exhale" with young adults at vacation Bible school one year, I remember hearing my married Pastor say he had confidence to "pull" (get) any woman he wanted, including Halle Berry. That day, my confidence was amplified even further, but in the wrong direction. This confidence opened the door to pornography, strip clubs and sexual experiments with promiscuous and seemingly innocent women.

I spent my first two years of college living on campus at East Texas Baptist University, where I played football for the University. The campus rules were fairly strict and set-up to create an environment that respected godly principles such as abstinence until marriage.

During the scheduled visitations the doors had to remain open and resident assistants monitored activity in each dorm room. However, males would find ways to break the rules by sneaking women into dormitories, finding dormant areas off campus and even renting cheap hotel rooms to proceed with sexual activities. No matter how tough the rules were, we found ways to bend the rules. In May 2002, I transferred to Morgan State University for my last few years of college and lived off campus. Within the first month of being in Baltimore, I was introduced to a young lady that was attending Morgan. She expressed interest in "showing me around". My car had not been transported to Maryland, so she kindly offered transportation. I accepted until my car arrived. After my car arrived, I continued to hang out with her forming a 'friendship without benefits'. One evening while at her home she began to throw herself at me, sexually. I literally ran. Although, I did not know the Bible well, I am sure it was the Holy Spirit that intervened, causing me to run. The Word of God says:

> Flee from sexual immorality. All other sins a person commits are outside the body, but whoever sins sexually, sins against their own body. Do you not know that your bodies are temples of the Holy Spirit, who is in you, whom you have received from God? You are not your own; you were bought at a price. Therefore honor God with your bodies.
>
> I Corinthians 6:18-20

I believe that this was the first time I heard from God regarding the importance of sexual purity. Yet, I didn't fully understand it and I didn't embrace it as I should have.

While at Morgan State I worked in the Youth & College Division of the National Association for the Advancement of Colored People (NAACP) and I was exposed to several prominent charismatic leaders in politics and business. I watched them and began to emulate them as I progressed in my college years. My role with the NAACP was seen as a position of power in the eyes of women at school and in the Chapters /Councils across the United States. I selectively took advantage of it. One of my male colleagues had a discussion with me about the quality of women that I was sexually involved with and encouraged me to connect the potential future possibility of an unintentional pregnancy. More specifically, he wanted to make sure I was taking into account the type of women I was connecting myself with. At the time, his logic seemed reasonable so I accepted it. Furthermore, I began to transition in "the game" even more after hearing a lesson on "supply & demand" in my economics class. Women became more attracted to me through my personal theory of "supply & demand". For example, if there was a woman on campus that all guys were attracted to, evidenced by their flocking to her, I ignored her. This would make her curious as to why I was not as interested as the other guys. She would then try to figure me out. This would increase my supply and reduce her demand for me, because I had her interested in me at that point. I used the same tactic with regard to sex. (Ladies, please watch out for these tactics). Based on these two points, you can imagine what my lifestyle was like. At one point, I had a different woman each night and even multiple in a night, having sex with 100+ women by the time I was a junior in college. I am not glorifying this lifestyle, but rather, I am condemning it. I was out of control and deceived. I am being transparent because you need to understand that sin has consequences and is not beneficial for anyone. I hurt a lot of people.

Growing up I was taught the importance of remaining connected to a church, so I attended church on Sunday mornings. I can remember having a conversation with one of my mentors, who was the youth Pastor at a church I attended. I told him I was having new feelings of remorse after having sex with women. Additionally, I experienced feelings of not wanting to be with them any longer after sexual intercourse. His response caught my attention, but it didn't provide any real guidance. After this conversation, I was moved to call women from my past to apologize for hurting them. These women laughed at me or disrespected me by hanging up in my face. I began to recognize that the way I treated women was wrong and I needed to reconcile my past. What if my father or male figures would have shown me the importance of treating women like God's daughters? What if I had the perspective that this young lady could be my daughter, sister or niece? Or what if this was my mother?

Later in my life I had an indelible encounter with God, which changed me forever. "Therefore, if anyone is in Christ, the new creation has come: The old has gone, the new is here!" (II Corinthians 5:17). I made mistakes earlier but God made me into a new creature, wiping all of the past sin from my life. After getting my relationship with God in order and allowing His Word to be the standard in my life, my life changed forever and I no longer felt the guilt of my past. I received a book entitled *"The Best Sex of My Life: a guide to purity"* from Ms. Joy Stevenson that provided me with even greater understanding of how God was transforming my life. I read the book, signed the sexual purity confession covenant within it on January 15, 2009. My commitment would be tested by different women interested in 'friends with benefits' opportunities and weekend sleepovers, but I continued to pursue this new life of purity. I committed myself to living a sexually pure life until marriage. As destiny would have it, my wife would be the woman who wrote the very book that helped to transform my mindset. Lindsay and I were married on October 30, 2010 and together we teach the importance of sexual purity through Worth The Wait Revolution (www.iamworthewaith.com). As a changed man, *The Best Sex of My Life* is not just a book series, but a fulfilling journey that I am experiencing exclusively with my wife, just as God ordained it. Only God can take my past mistakes, ignorance, sexual sins and reckless behavior and use it to bring healing to others. Do not let your past define you! My name is Gareth P. Warren; I don't smoke, drink or place anything that causes harm in my body and I WAS WORTH THE WAIT!

Confessions of a Sexual Purity Revolution, Part I

THE LADIES

And they have overcome (conquered) him by means of the
blood of the Lamb and by the utterance of their testimony . . .
Revelation 12:11a

<u>Confession:</u> By Lynnea Johnson

I am not embarrassed. I am not ashamed of the Gospel of Jesus Christ and to Him be all the glory! This was not always the case; I used to strive to fit in. I did not always know that God had a plan for my life regarding sex and my sexuality. I remember like it was yesterday. In the ninth grade, a few of the girls gathered to talk around the school track, in gym class. The topic of sex came up. Many shared their experiences with sex and how many times they had done it and how good it felt. I remember being very quiet. I couldn't relate to what they were talking about. I did not have these stories to share. One of them turned to me and said ". . . girl you don't know what you're missing". I thought to myself, "Missing? There is something that I'm missing out on? Will this make me more popular? Will more boys like me?" These conversations did not end. It seemed like everyone was having sex and something was wrong with me because I wasn't! Well, this was one of the many lies of the devil that I believed. No one had really told me that my worth was more than what this world had to offer. I remember what it felt like the first time a boy looked me up and down like he wanted me. I also remember the first time a boy grabbed my butt at a party, and the first time a boy told me he wanted to have sex with me. The first time a boy asked me if I was a virgin and I lied. I told him that I was 'nowhere close to one'. This attention made me feel good. I felt wanted. I felt sexy.

You see, I used to fear not being accepted; not belonging, not being loved. These feelings caused me to make decisions. Decisions that I can say I no longer really regret, because God has used them and my testimony for His glory! I pray that others learn from my decisions. I was fifteen years old when I lost my virginity. I remember knowing right then that something was not right, but another part of me was SO excited to tell my friends that were already doing it, so that I could join them in their conversation. I thought that this would bring me and my 'first real boyfriend' closer. Well, that relationship ended about three months later. From that point until college, I thought it was normal and expected to have sex with your boyfriend. Thank God that I did not have that many boyfriends! After learning that these sexual relationships could not make me whole, God drew me back to Himself and I made the decision to wait until my marriage at the age of twenty-one. I finally made the commitment to wait for my husband! Has everyday been easy? NO! Have I fallen and thought lustfully about a man and had other sexual struggles? YES! But God has forgiven me and kept me.

There was even a season after I made a commitment of purity that I was very ashamed and embarrassed of sharing my sexual purity stance. I was ashamed of being a content single woman and walking in the purpose He has for my life. Thankfully, a dear friend told me about Worth The Wait Revolution and the first event I went to was the Gala in 2008. This was honestly the first time I saw young men, women and teens that were sexually pure, talking about it in public, and THEY WERE FLY! I laugh now, but that's really how I felt. I thought, ". . . oh my goodness Lord, this thing is real and others are doing this and they have style and flavor too. They make sexual purity look good! I have got to get connected with this great move of God". Since then, I have seen the hand of God on this ministry and on my life. Worth The Wait Revolution and Dr. Lindsay Warren have made such an impact in my life and now I am excited to share with family, friends, co-workers, the world! I have also learned that there are rewards to being obedient with sexual purity. It is not a life sentence. I fully believe that if you have the desire to be married God will manifest it. Moreover, I thank God for showing me that only HE can make me whole; not popularity, not my 'boo' and not sex. I have GREAT expectations in the Lord regarding my life, relationships, ministry and marriage!

Confession: By Rhesa Riley

People always say that men are primarily attracted to what they see which is why they become mesmerized at the sight of a woman, but I can totally attest to the fact that it is not just men. Growing up I used to like the tall, athletic guys; curly hair, cute face. This was typical for me, at least until the tenth grade when my eyes were opened. In tenth grade, I had a friend on the football team and boy oh boy was he ripped. I would sit in class and just stare at everything from his shoulders to his calves to everything! Believe me when I say that I did not even need to see ole boy naked because I could very easily make up a fantasy on my own. At this point I will fast forward to a birthday I had a few years back, after I became a Christian. A friend invited me to the strip club. Now I knew it was definitely something I should not do, but the draw and the desire had always been there to go. I was so drawn to men's bodies it seemed to be a place I would enjoy, and enjoy it, I did. After my first initial time of going, it gave me this high, something to look forward to that was fun, entertaining and expensive. I was a student at the time and could not afford these visits to the strip club, but somehow I made my way there at least once a week. (At times, I was there twice a week to see some of the sexiest men I had ever seen shake, flip and grind on all kinds of women.) Unfortunately, my addiction to the strip club escalated to the point where it was the only thing I could look forward to during the week. Nothing else could match its intensity or level of excitement. I had friends telling me to stop going. I started lying about my whereabouts and even started borrowing money to throw to these men. My pivotal moment during this time was when I had decided that I was going to pay $200 for a private party with my favorite stripper, just me and him. I was all set to go and you better believe my body was literally on fire for this man. I am a VIRGIN! Nevertheless, somewhere in my mind, if I ended up having sex with that man it was going to be alright with me. Consequently, my money never arrived on time. The private party never happened. Yet, I knew even the sins I was committing in my mind and outwardly, that God wanted me to step away. However, I just couldn't. I never knew I could be so weak, lustful, or greedy. The more I went, the hornier I got. I fooled myself into thinking the strip club was an outlet, but it was really only cheapening my ideals about sex.

During this time I had been taking a class called, "Wholeness With God" and it definitely helped to eventually pull me away. One of the last times I went to the strip club, I remember sitting in a chair starring at this woman climb all over my favorite stripper and God showed me a flash forward of what I would become if I did not get a hold of myself and let this go. Needless to say, it wasn't a pretty sight and not long after I let it go. The desire to go did not stop right away, but in this God also showed me how important it was to have pure thoughts and pure conversation. He showed me how all of those things drove me and kept me at the strip club every week for more than six months. Since that time, I have been committed to keeping the "TV" screen of my mind clear so as to never have to go back to that sin again. God is awesome and I am thankful that He delivered me. I know He is keeping me and preparing me for the man He has set aside for me.

Confession: By Marquita Brooks

I am the product of a teen mother. My birth father was only in my life for the first year. Then, he made the decision to no longer bear that responsibility and decided to leave me and my mother. After the separation, my mother married a man whom I titled father, because when I reached the age to identify a man as a father, he was present. Unfortunately, he became physically abusive towards my mom. This made life at home very difficult at times. Eventually, my mom made the decision to be free from the abuse and divorced him.

Around the age of eight, my birth father reemerged into my life, and a year later my mom married him. What should have been a joyous occasion for most was a very emotional time for me. Not far into the marriage my father started using drugs, which caused many problems at home. He would leave home and be gone for days and sometimes even weeks. This left me confused about his absence and made me feel unwanted at times. I watched my mom go through years of frustration, which lead her to be overly protective because she didn't want me to go down the same road.

Though I had been raised in the church, I don't remember hearing that my body was the temple of the Holy Spirit while growing up. In 2003, I went to college and started partying and drinking, and engaged in sexual activity. I even smoked weed a couple of times. I found myself living a reckless lifestyle and was using those things as outlets to fill the void that I was feeling on the inside. I would try to make myself feel better about what I was doing, but deep down inside I felt convicted. Even still I went against those convictions I felt and gave into my flesh. This lifestyle that I had been living had

43

me in bondage, but God continued to keep me. In 2005, I made the choice to be abstinent but I still struggled with being sexually pure. I thought that as long as I wasn't having sex I could do whatever else I wanted to do, but being sexual pure means more than being abstinent.

In 2008, I made the decision to cut all sexual ties; I knew changes needed to be made. I was left feeling hopeless, lonely, and unwanted. A year later I met a young lady that told me about having a true relationship with Christ. This led me to truly begin seeking God more in my life. I had such a yearning to know Him, as well as, please Him. I even began exploring those past hurts and pains, which caused me to still harbor ill feelings towards my dad. I realized I could not grow deeper in God, while holding on to all those past hurts. I finally broke down and surrendered to God, I wanted to be free from the emptiness and the emotional effects of the lifestyle I had lived.

Now I am proud to say that God has turned my life around and removed the bitterness from my heart. He taught me how to release those things that had me in bondage. I had to forgive myself and others. I am now active in ministry and continuing my education in Christian Leadership. It amazes me how Christ chooses us before we decide to come to Him; He continues to come after us even when we continue to turn our backs on Him. He truly desires for us to become whole and complete, lacking nothing. The road to sexual purity hasn't been easy but I know it's what God requires of me, and my desire is to please Him. I AM WORTH THE WAIT!!! I thank God for Dr. Lindsay and The Worth the Wait Revolution for the encouragement and upholding the standard of purity.

Confession: By Yvonne Orji, Model/Comedienne/Actress/Writer

Follow the Leader:

It's been over a decade since I first met Dr. Lindsay as a freshman at The George Washington University during a meeting at Word Up! Bible Study. I'll never forget when I heard her speak. Here she was: beautiful, a doctor, driving a Benz, living in a NICE condo IN DC . . . and a virgin?! Scrruuuummphh! (Pumping breaks). Come again? I remember sitting there thinking, "What she got? A disease? I don't get it!" After attending a few more sessions and getting to know "Dr. L" personally, I began to admire her all the more. You see, I too was waiting to have sex . . . but for all the wrong reasons. When I was thirteen, I witnessed my Primary Care Physician in distress because she had to call the mother of a sixteen year old and inform her of her daughter's pregnancy. I knew about patient-doctor confidentiality, but evidently missed the memo about it being null and void for a minor. Right then and there, I made a decision that NOBODY was calling Mama Orji to tell her NOTHING about a baby and me! (I like my life!). So I decided that I would wait to have sex until I turned eighteen.

Jokes On Me:

God had other plans. I started college when I was seventeen. I met Dr. L (and her virgin self—*sucks teeth* & rolls eye* :-)) when I was seventeen. Are you seeing the connection? Now at twenty-nine and still a virgin, my reasons for waiting are no longer because I'm afraid of my momma, (Don't get me wrong . . . I'm still a little scared of her backhand . . . just a lil' bit), but because of being able to closely watch Dr. L live a life of integrity, walk in purpose and receive the blessing. As a result of "imitating those, who through faith and patience, inherited the promise," I've been led to proudly proclaim my stance on abstinence through my own clothing line, which was birth directly from Dr. L's ministry.

Pass It On:

Has it always been easy to wait? Emphatically NO! Do I sometimes get the urge to "wanna get some?!" Of course (Don't act like you don't also . . . Yeah you!). But knowing that my obedience pleases God and the fruit of my decision HAS TO BE GOOD, makes the wait well worth it! I think the life of Steve Jobs, founder of Apple and inventor of the "iEverything" has shown the world that one idea, one spark, one individual can ignite a social revolution. I firmly believe that Dr. Lindsay's passion for restoring God's original purpose for sex and purity can equally set ablaze a much needed sexual revolution! My Pastor, Dr. Michael A. Freeman, frequently poses this question: "If you are the only Jesus people will ever see, is God in trouble?" My answer? "Not on my watch!" As a professional comedian, I have been given a platform to not only entertain, but also share my testimony. I can't tell you how many times after a show, people come up to me and say, "You're a virgin? But you're so cool?!" Their dismay does two things for me. On the one hand, it makes me laugh because it's the exact same look of awe and puzzlement I had upon hearing

Dr. L share her testimony. Secondly, it lets me know that I am doing exactly what I'm called to do: change the image and perception of what it means to be a Christian and live a life that pleases the Father! Thanks Dr. L for showing me how to "Pay the Revolution forward!"

Confession: By Nicole Miller

I lost my virginity when I was seventeen years old. Although I wasn't a born again believer, I did often pray to God and experienced answered prayer. (He is so merciful). The night I lost my virginity, I could sense that He did not want this to happen. He did not want me to cross this very sacred threshold. So much rebellion and anger was rooted in my heart that I told God I didn't care what He thought. I wanted what I wanted and was going to do what I wanted to do. I'm sure most would agree that you don't just 'have sex'. No! There are many steps that lead to pre-marital sex, regardless of one's age. I can remember being a child and involved in sexual activity with other children in my neighborhood and school. I see now a very calculated plan from the enemy to infiltrate my generation with lust, fornication, and sexual immorality. Masturbation became a serious issue during my pre-teen years, and still haunts me to this day. Watching late night sexually explicit movies and listening to R&B/secular rap, only watered the seeds which were planted in my heart at such a young age. So, by the time I hit seventeen years old, I was deceived to believe that I was ready to make such a life changing decision involving my body. I had barely known the lucky guy, as we had only been together for a few weeks. He never took me out on a date, bought me roses, or treated me like a real girlfriend. For him, it was just sex. For me, it was about a need to feel wanted and loved. A few days afterward, I found out that he had sex with his ex-girlfriend the very next day, after we had been together. Sadly though, I still stayed with him for a few more months. (In reflection, my obvious lack of self worth stared right back at me.)

There were a string of guys before this one, and a few after him. Many of them I was physical with, even if we didn't have sex. But I didn't really fall in love until I was almost eighteen. We were together for four years and we were sexually involved. Even though the relationship didn't work out, Christ had His hand on us. During the course of the relationship we became born-again and received conviction about living a life of sexual purity. After the relationship ended, the Lord gave me an incredible grace to walk in holiness in this area.

It's been almost seven years since my last sexual encounter. There have been some serious temptations and close calls, but God is faithful. I believe the key to experiencing this type of grace is, surrendering to God. We are not able to resist temptation unless we first submit and surrender to Him. Then He, through us, resists the devil, and the devil must flee (James 4:7). I have experienced His forgiveness, His grace, His love, and His sustaining strength. Through the resurrection of Christ we not only have salvation, but we have victory. As He overcame, we now overcome.

Confession: By Shirelle, Author of "Sinless Sex"

Re-Virginized

I would love to say that I waited for marriage before I gave up my goodies, but that is not my testimony. I, like many others who didn't know their value, settled for the handsome hunk with the chiseled chest and bulging biceps, on many occasions. Yet, something was missing. It wasn't until my thirty-something days that I realized what it was and who I was. A royal priesthood, created in the image of God. A flawed diamond, yet I still had sparkle.

So I was summoned to appear at the Trinity Court on charges of lust and fornication. I raised my hand, "Guilty as charged your Honor," was my plea. Hoping to get a sentence for misdemeanors and not felonies, the Judge said it didn't matter because it was all the same. I pleaded for grace and mercy. The Judge granted me probation before judgment and scheduled my reappearance in one year and said that if there was no remorse which would be evident by my lifestyle, I would be sentenced to a mediocre average life, unable to experience Heaven on Earth, postponed purpose, and a destiny forever on detour. However, if at my reappearance I was delivered from my flesh and submitted to His spirit, I would experience the abundant life, protection from the devourer (Satan), a prosperous purpose, a divine destiny, and to top it off, the best sex of my life, in due season. I bargained with the Judge and I said, "Okay, but I like the sex I'm having now so you are going to have to do it for me, I can't do it by myself." He said, "Fine, I'll send my Son." I asked one more request. "Your Honor, can He save that issue for last, the fornication one, because I have quite a few more habits that He can work on first before we get to that one if you don't mind. My accomplices name is Stallion, so I'm sure you can understand. Thank you for your consideration."

So as I submitted and while His Son was working with me, I didn't even notice the misdemeanors and felonies (sins) were dwindling away, soon to be memories. Little by little, one by one He was weaning me away from those things that I thought I couldn't live without. My reappearance date was fast approaching so I did a self evaluation. No more smoking, drinking, pornography, and by-golly-gee, no more lust and fornication!

I was excited for my reappearance at Trinity Court. "Your Honor, it is with my pleasure that I come humbly to you to ask your forgiveness for my past transgressions. It was not as hard as I thought to change the things that displeased you thanks to you sending your Son to help me. You will be happy to know that even though I wouldn't give up my Stallion for three ponies, I did give him up for my one God. I am officially Re-Virginized." The Judge replied, "My daughter, you are forgiven. You have met the conditions to get the provisions. Enjoy your blessings that have been stored up just for you. Now go and sin no more."

Confession: By Johnetta L. Howard

After joining Worth The Wait Revolution in 2007, my whole life changed. I always knew I wanted to wait for marriage to have sex, but my role models and examples were scarce. I felt so alone, and consequently, I was slipping. I was doing everything but sex; involved in impure relationships with no purpose. Worth The Wait Revolution gave me so much encouragement to walk this walk and walk it right. I thought because I wasn't having sex, I was in good standing with God. I quickly realized after seeing how God viewed sexual purity that I had a lot of mess to clean up in my personal life. I started attending events, volunteering, modeling, and most importantly reading *"The Best Sex of My Life: a Guide To Purity"* and applying what I was learning to my personal walk. I always had standards, but now my standards were getting higher and lining up with the word of God. Before I met Dr. Lindsay, I had never seen a beautiful, young, intelligent, successful woman of God who was a virgin and living a pure life. I had something to strive for. Her ministry and lifestyle made me want to step up my game for God and live a life of purity and excellence. I didn't realize how valuable and priceless I was. I was giving too much of myself away to too many people. Not realizing that ALL of me was to be kept for God and shared only with one man, my husband. I am so thankful that God led me to this ministry and Dr. Lindsay because now I know the truth and importance of living a sexually pure life.

It was such a struggle for me to hold on to my virginity in college and as a young adult. My confidence was in my body and beauty, rather than the word of God. I had no idea what God said about me or why He commanded me to wait. It seemed so unfair that my relationships only lasted a few months because I wouldn't go all the way. It felt even worse to give bits and pieces of myself away over and over again leading me to the same broken heart every time. I was told that men couldn't wait. It was impossible for them, so compromise was necessary for my relationships to last. Even after being saved, I was still on this emotional rollercoaster. I was breaking God's heart by breaking off pieces of myself to give to my "boyfriends". Marriage seemed so far off, but my dream of the "perfect" marriage and husband was still deep inside my heart. I truly believed I would have the "fairytale" life but I wasn't sure how to get there or how to make the time go by faster in the meantime. I had my "last" boyfriend a few years ago and he kept telling me he loved me and that I was his wife. I disagreed. I didn't feel the same way about him immediately, but eventually convinced myself, that he was my husband because he was so persistent. This relationship only lasted 6 months and was very impure. Love was confused with lust. One day, he ended the relationship without explanation. It hurt so badly because I thought this was "it". I became fed up with selling myself short just to have the title of "girlfriend". I became disgusted with giving my all to someone who was temporary, while expecting a lifelong dream. I was focusing on a relationship with a lust trap, instead of focusing on getting to know my first and only true love: God. I was living an unfulfilled single life. Once again, my heart was broken into a million pieces. God put it back together again. I finally made the decision to do things the pure way or no way at all. I deserved more and God told me I was worth more. The next man I met was my answered prayer. From the beginning, I told him of my high standards and commitment to purity. We went through 4 stages: friendship, courtship, engagement, and now marriage. He was never my "boyfriend". Our relationship always had a purpose. He waited for me and I waited for him. We got married on November 20, 2010 and our wedding night was priceless. It was everything that God promised me and more. I'm not just talking about the sex, but

I'm talking about the intimacy, trust, true love, and commitment, (all of which I had never experienced before). There was no guilt or shame, because God said 'it' was okay. We were able to give ourselves to each other for the first time and there is no better feeling in the world. We are still walking in purity in our marriage by protecting our ear gates, and eye gates from pornography, lust, and the pressures of extra-marital relationships. We are also completely honest with each other, praying with and for each other. Our children will be raised in purity. We have set a great foundation of purity for them and have led the way for generations to come.

Confession: By Cheryl Thomas

THE BEST KEPT SECRET

Everyone loves a juicy secret. It has the elements we all love: mystery, intrigue and mystique. For most, it's not really the secret that we crave knowing, it's the feeling of superiority we get when we feel we have something others don't have or possess insight and information that is widely esteemed as privileged.

While everyone loves secrets, there are few people who can actually keep them. They are often widely shared without thought. Have you ever told someone something that was so personal and private only to hear that person betrayed your trust? Your secret is out and trust is gone.

As quiet as it's kept, our virginity is supposed to be kept like a secret and only shared with our spouse. It's not a cheap toy to be given to anyone who wants to play. It is a prized possession that is reserved for the confines of marriage.

But how do you keep such a great secret to yourself when the world tells you it's okay to share your secret with someone who you're "in love" with, regardless of whether you are married or not? It's not an easy thing to do.

Forty-three years is a long time to keep a secret, but I'm proud to say that I am still keeping my secret. I haven't always been able to say I was proud. In my teens and early twenties, I was anything but proud. I was embarrassed.

I wanted to be one of the cool girls with the attention of all the guys. I wanted to have guys look at me the way they looked at my friends. Oh, the naiveté of youth. I didn't know then that those young ladies were offering something I wasn't willing to give up. I wasn't willing to give up my secret, my virginity.

Now don't get me wrong. I was tempted just like anyone else. Yes, temptation. No matter how "saved" we are, how much we say we love the Lord or how much we claim total deliverance from every evil, temptation will rear its ugly head and make us EARN the right to that proclamation.

However, the temptation wasn't really about sex for me. It was about acceptance. Although there was extreme peer pressure from friends and classmates to join them and indulge in sex before marriage, my fear of God constrained me.

You see, I was raised in a hellfire and brimstone church where everything was wrong. It pains me to admit that initially I didn't abstain from sex because I loved the Lord. I abstained because I didn't want to go to hell!

However, the enemy is a trickster and a master in the art of subtle deceit. He didn't come right at me and tell me sex was not a sin, he suggested smaller indulgences that weren't necessarily sins, but weren't profitable for my growth.

I experienced a little inappropriate touch here, or a little touch there. But something in my heart wouldn't let me accept those encounters as okay. If it wasn't against God's will, why did I feel so bad in my heart? If it was really okay, why did it bother me so?

It bothered me because I knew it bothered God. It bothered me because I knew I was better than that and that I deserved more. It bothered me because my love for God had finally outgrown my fear of hell.

Over the years I've learned that it is our love for God that constrains us much better than fear ever could. It is this love that causes us to forego our desires because we want His will. It is this love that compels us to keep His secret when the world tells us to share.

The Creator of the universe has given us a great gift and asked that we hold this secret until marriage. Not as a punishment to us, but for our benefit. May we all, from this day forward decide that our secret is worth the wait.

Confession: By Jaelin Blyther

I am sixteen years old, and I am a virgin. Since attending my first event in 2006, Worth The Wait Revolution (WTWR) has been a big eye opener and life changer for me. The runway and confession events show me that WTWR is more than a title, it's a lifestyle. It's helpful for me to see the struggles other people have overcome and I realize that they would not have overcome without God. HE is truly amazing. Dr. Lindsay Warren has helped to change my thinking for the better. She is a compassionate minister and has taught me to be a leader. Her positive attitude and openness about sharing her past experiences has been helpful to hear because I have learned from her mistakes instead of making them myself. Before she got married, she practiced exactly what she is teaching. The events she holds are fun and exciting and they're easy to learn from. Great questions are always answered on her sexual purity panels. The very questions that run through the minds of teens get addressed and it's not just someone spitting bible verses at you. Being abstinent is a great way to fully understand that as a young lady, my body is the temple of God and I am a virtuous woman. It is also a way to stay protected from diseases and any accidental pregnancies. I appreciate everything that Dr. Lindsay has taught me. My name is Jaelin Blyther and I AM WORTH THE WAIT.

Confession: By Heavenly Beloved

"IM JUST KEEPING IT REAL"

At the age of seventeen, I made a vow to myself and God that I would make a decision to remain celibate until marriage. Never a naturally promiscuous woman, I had no idea about the struggle that lie ahead. In my mind, I knew that celibacy would be the least of my worries. Needless to say, I was totally wrong.

About six months into my journey, I met what seemed to be the man of my dreams. He was handsome, hardworking, went to church and loved God. I won the jackpot!! Even in our times of temptation, we would read the Bible together to find scriptures that would remind us of why we were waiting to have sex. Yet, the temptation grew. Reflecting back, I know that the only reason he was celibate was to make me happy. Consequently, he couldn't keep his hands to himself and honestly, I didn't want him to. Before we knew it, we were having sex.

This failure was the beginning of my downward spiral. The former carefree, spunky, center of attention person I once was had now become a woman who was plagued with guilt, shame, and inadequacy. Not only had I disappointed myself, but I had disappointed God. Since I already felt like a failure, this caused me to give up. I had already had sex with him anyway, so I might as well continue to have sex. I had more, and more and more sex, until eventually I ended up pregnant!

"Eighteen years old and pregnant? This was totally not my plan! I don't even know who I am anymore!" These were all of the thoughts running through my mind. I didn't know where to turn. I didn't want to tell anyone because I was ashamed and scared. After sharing this story with my boyfriend, he expressed to me that he didn't want a baby. I had already experienced that rejection from my own father, so I decided there was absolutely no way that I would bring a child into this world with a father that didn't want to be one. I searched for abortion clinics in the area and I went to get the 'procedure'. When I arrived, they gave me an ultrasound to see how far along I was in the pregnancy. My nurse bent to the floor intentionally (I believe), and as soon as she bent over, I was able to see the ultrasound. After that, I just couldn't go through with it. I paid for the sonogram and left the office. I hoped that the picture of our unborn child would change my boyfriend's heart. But his heart did not change. I went back, got the abortion and was numb for weeks to come.

For several weeks, I blanked it out. Then, I experienced depression. I began to literally hate myself. I felt unloved and unlovable. I just knew God was done with me. Every day, I prayed that God would help me get out of the relationship. I knew I could not do it on my own. But with God's help, I was eventually able to walk away.

After spending some time with God and rediscovering who I was, I began to build my confidence again. I now understood that God gave me guidelines outlined within the scriptures, for my benefit. I felt empowered and strong. The only thing left to do was to share my story about the abortion, so that I could shed those layers of guilt and shame. Once I shared my story for the first time, publically, I knew that I was healed. Not only was my life changed forever, but others were transformed.

Most importantly, I rededicated my life to God, and recommitted myself to truly remain celibate until marriage. The difference this time around is that I no longer have confidence in my own ability to remain pure. I acknowledge that only God has kept me. I don't put myself in situations that I know I can't handle. Know your limits and stay within those boundaries.

Confession: **By India Pittman**

Living Multiple Lives

Everyone called me the "church girl". Early on, my mother told me I would not be allowed to date until I graduated from college. I didn't do well with authority, so I became very defiant. As I got older I continued to defy my mom; Talking to boys on the phone at night, going out with friends and meeting up with boys in various places. My freshman year of high school, I dated a guy that turned out to be bi-sexual. My sophomore year, I willingly lost my virginity at fifteen, (one week before my sixteenth birthday); to a guy I had only been dating for two weeks. Although, my parents always told me to remain a virgin until marriage, no one ever explained exactly why. So, after my first time, sex became routine. Almost two months into the relationship, I contracted 'Mono' (Mononucleosis) from my boyfriend. While I was at home recovering, he was at school dating another girl. The whole experience caused me to be resentful towards males. I started talking to other guys, and then I met this girl. She introduced me to the homosexual lifestyle. I was never really into girls, but I did it to get revenge for "my first" and every other male that ever treated me badly. Most of all, I wanted to get back at my mom for not "allowing" me to date. But, being a lesbian wasn't for me and I finally cut her off. I started getting really stressed out about the life I was living.

One of my friends introduced me to cigarettes. That became my release. My senior year in high school, I had stopped smoking, but I felt like I needed more. I had sex with a few of my friends, and then started looking for guys to fulfill my needs. I met a guy and he became my boyfriend for almost three years. He introduced me to more sex, weed, alcohol, and everything else under the sun. Even in this mess, I was still going to church every Sunday. Eventually, my boyfriend cheated on me. A month before I left for college I had reached my breaking point with him and ended the relationship. I knew it was time for me to just live holy. I needed to leave my past behind. I stopped smoking, drinking, and having sex. I started journaling, reading my bible and praying more.

I got to college, went to my first party and I started partying, smoking and drinking again. I went home one weekend and fell back into a trap with my ex-boyfriend. Back at school I tried so hard not to go back to the lifestyle that I lived before, but sex still had a hold on me. I was involved with a guy that was off campus and he treated me like his sex toy. Then there was a senior on campus that I started talking to. I became hungry for his affection and attention. Strangely, one night, I was with him and I felt like I was going to be raped. I could tell by the way he was looking at me and the way he was holding me. He pinned me down on the bed and tried to take my pants off, but I kept saying no. I got away from him. I cried all night. I didn't even sleep. The next morning I left and didn't call him for almost a month. Before the last day of the semester he called me over. We talked and I feel asleep. I woke up the next morning beside him and Holy Spirit said "FLEE!" That was the clearest I have EVER heard God's voice about anything; it shook me to my core. Without any question, I got out of the bed and left without saying goodbye. When I left his house that day, I left the soul tie, him, and every other sin that had me bound.

Happy Ending

I rededicated my life to Christ, began to read my Word again, and really started to thirst for God like never before. I haven't looked back since. That night was really a wakeup call for me. I have been celibate for over two years now, and I am saving myself for my husband. I'm taking advantage of this 'single life', really getting to know God and pursuing my dreams as a young woman of God.

<u>Confession:</u> By Denise

I have struggled with premarital sex for nearly ten years. It all started my freshman year, when I met this intelligent, charming young man. At this point in life, I had encountered many attractive men but there was just something intriguing about this one guy. He was the most intellectually stimulating guy I had ever met. I would always smile when I saw him. He just did something to me. The very first time he asked me out, I was hesitant. I am not sure if it was nerves or something else. I decided to go and we had a great time. Over the next few months, we began to get to know each other and spent more time together. One night after dinner, we were sitting in the car and I had one of the strangest experiences of my life. I felt someone urging me not to pursue a relationship with this guy. It felt like a major warning telling me to get far away from him. I believe that someone urging me was God. It was a very odd experience, but it was one of the clearest messages I had ever received. It was a warning;

Warning about a path of pain and self-destruction. Unfortunately, I did not heed that warning from God. The next few years included the introduction to premarital sex, poor academic performance, and damaged relationships with family and friends. Life goals and aspirations were totally lost or delayed. I went through years of guilt, depression, and even suicidal thoughts. To this day, I have not fully recovered. I read "The Best Sex of My Life: a Guide To Purity", but I still struggle with sexual temptation today. Honestly, I opened up a door of destruction that requires major determination, prayer, and faith for real deliverance, everyday.

Confession: By Jennifer Black

I no longer wanted to be a virgin at the age of thirteen. I remember being made fun of on the school bus for being a virgin. I felt so embarrassed by my peers. I didn't really have anyone to encourage me to remain abstinent, except for my mom. So at the age of thirteen (almost fourteen), I lost my virginity to a guy that I should have never lost it to. I was so proud of myself for no longer being labeled the "V" word.

For the next three years of my life, (until the age of sixteen), I was sexually active and very unhappy. I didn't sleep with many guys but nevertheless, I was doing things I shouldn't have been doing. I kept all these things from my mom who was a strong Christian. My mom would constantly pray for me. At the age of fourteen, I gave my life to Christ at a conference featuring Evangelist R. W. Schambach. Yet, I still struggled with the things I had to give up. At the age of fifteen, I was filled with the Holy Ghost. I experienced something I've never had before; the peace and love of God. I was transformed into a new creature in Christ and I knew it.

Unfortunately, I got involved with a guy that I had always wanted to be with. He was the last guy I slept with. He was my stronghold. I remember watching Juanita Bynum's "No More Sheets" during this time. I cried out even more for deliverance and finally felt that God was answering my prayers. I called my boyfriend to tell him that I couldn't sleep with him any longer because I wanted to please God. Yet, I still found myself calling him from time to time, even though it was evident that he was now disgusted with me. I was living a different lifestyle. I eventually threw away pictures and clothes that reminded me of him.

One day, I drove past his house, but never got out the car. The Holy Spirit arrested me with so much conviction. I knew I should not have come to his house and I was lead to turn around. For many years I didn't even look over in the direction of his home or drive in the area of his home. I guarded myself. I feared that I would be drawn back.

Not long after this incident, the Holy Spirit took me through a season of transformation. During this time, I wasn't allowed to give my number to a guy. I experienced what some would call a "Man Fast". My emotional life was out of order. He had to restore my soul; mind, will and emotions. He showed me my destiny. Now I encourage others to walk in the freedom made available to us through Jesus Christ.

Confession: By Latoya Keith

My journey back to a lifestyle of sexual purity was unique, yet familiar. I was raised in strict but godly atmosphere. My home life consisted of family and church. My father was an ordained deacon and my mother was an excellent example of a Proverbs 31 wife. However, when it came to open discussion on sex, it was a taboo subject. Teaching from home only touched on the Biblical principle that sex outside marriage was wrong. I recall in middle school, having to sneak into health class just to learn additional information about sex. My father's response when I requested clarification on topics I'd learned in class was: 1) stay away from boys, 2) dating was off-limits, and 3) there would be no phones calls, or outings with the opposite sex. These guidelines were strictly enforced, as it wasn't until college when I had my first official date. As a seventeen year old virgin in college, I was challenged in many ways (i.e. parties, drinking, etc). I continued on the righteous path, but without fully understanding who I was in Christ, I eventually detoured. After graduation, I joined the U.S. Air Force as an officer and went to my first assignment. I still didn't drink or party, but I did have my first encounter with oral sex. It was troubling for me initially, since I wasn't sure if I was still considered a virgin after the act. Upon confiding in close friends, I was told that this act was just foreplay, and that I was still a virgin in the physiological sense. This one act opened the door to frequent masturbation and seemly innocent "bumping and grinding". Eventually, I lost my virginity at twenty-five years old to my very first boyfriend. When I shared the news with my mother, she resentfully asked if I was still her daughter. Condemnation set in and that opened the door to promiscuity. My boyfriend and I eventually split. I, then, found myself in a rebound relationship. When that fell through, I entered a new relationship with a guy I thought was for me. My flesh remained weak without the Word of God and renewing of my mind. I knew what the Word of God said, but my flesh craved more. Even though I proclaimed I was a Christian and loved God, the fruit was definitely lacking in that area of my life.

Upon getting my fourth assignment back in the U.S., I finally came face to face with who I had become. It was not the virtuous woman that my parents had decreed over me years ago. I came to myself; had an intimate talk with Father God and reassessed all of the godly goals that I once had for my life while growing up. My desires for a husband, children and career, was being jeopardized by my choices and the reckless path I was on. Finally, I stopped doing what I knew was wrong in my heart. Within two months of returning to the US, I obtained a renewed strength from God and got back on track spiritually. God blessed my obedience and I met my husband. Please believe, the overall process was crucial, but throughout our courting we remained abstinent, in spite of our backgrounds and previous choices. I truly believe that it was through the Worth the Wait Revolution in its entirety (the ministry book, events, our active participation) and just being under the Word of God at Spirit of Faith Christian Center that made this new walk of purity, attainable and sustainable. People ask us, how we overcame. We tell them it's only by God's grace, His mercy and our uncompromising will, that we made it through the process. So, for ALL those that may be thinking," . . . I can't do it" or "it's too late for me", or "God won't forgive me"; we and many others of the Revolution are living examples that it is possible. God will bless your diligence and give you the strength to make it through to the very end. I'm Latoya Keith and yes, I was Worth the Wait!

Confession: By Vanessa Fleeton

My sexual experience started at the tender age of fourteen. I found myself fighting over this boy in the high school halls. I exchanged my virginity for a little attention and a pair of shell toe Adidas sneakers (a gift from my first boyfriend). I went on to sleep with many men to fill the void left by my absent father, despite a mother who did the best she knew how. I was an honor roll student, but school couldn't teach me self-worth. I didn't love myself. At age nineteen, I started having a series of abortions. By age twenty-one, I had my last one after I was put out of the house by my mom. I was accomplished academically, (received two degrees and worked for the federal government), but I was still empty inside; feeling unloved and unwanted. I was married in 2000 and divorced by 2005. We rushed into marriage and I didn't even know what marriage was, because I never saw a good example. Well, long story short, he was the last man that I had sex with. Glory to God! I made a promise to wait for my husband (as my purity ring states). I had a close call in 2010 (kissing and hugging), but I passed the test. I have an on/off relationship with my father, which is not so demanding because God filled that void a long time ago. My renewed life is due to my eleven year membership at the Soul Factory church. I also credit Worth the Wait Revolution because I see that sexual purity can be sassy (not sexy) and there are people out there who are waiting. Hopefully, my mess can serve as a message to help someone go a different way than what I chose. In spite of my past, I'm currently successfully single and I AM WORTH THE WAIT.

Confession: By Robin Rogers

August 2012, I celebrated five years of being single and celibate. However, for twenty-three years, I remained with a man that had multiple affairs. He was verbally, emotionally and mentally abusive. It all ended that September when he left for work and never returned home. He decided for us, that it was over.

How would I explain this to my then, fifteen year old daughter, and seventeen year old son? I had two great kids. Both were (are) still virgins. This was not about them. They didn't deserve this. I had a choice to make. For the next six months that followed the walk-out, I went through a season of depression and loneliness. A rebound relationship was not the cure. I had work to do from the inside, out. Immediately, I began to guard my heart, guard my eyes and my ears. Anything that would gratify my flesh became obsolete. I praised God for protecting me during the prior twenty-three year relationship, and not allowing me to contract a single STD.

Instead of blaming my spouse, I had to ask God to show me areas that I needed to work on. Internal work had to be done. The reveal was painful, but the journey was transforming. Rejection, shame and embarrassment were very real challenges. There was more work to do internally. I began investing in and doing more for myself. At the end of two years, I knew that God had done a work in me. I was healed of the anger and bitterness in my heart towards certain family members. My healing started a rippling effect of healing for my son and daughter, as well. Encouraging them to forgive their father, and walk in love, didn't happen until they saw me open my heart and demonstrate what I had been preaching to them. Instantly, I saw the power of God transform our hearts.

Part of my daily confession was that my daughter and son would remain virgins until their wedding day. I also made daily faith confessions about the type of spouse they would marry. During the two years of processing through the pain, we had Dr. Lindsay visit our former church, with the Worth The Wait message of sexual purity. My son and daughter now had another identifiable role model, (besides me), proving that abstinence could be obtained. We purchased her book and t-shirts. It blessed me to watch my daughter proudly sport her "I AM WORTH THE WAIT" shirt and read her book. After I read the book, my stance for celibacy intensified. Today, I am still rebuilding my life, but I am enjoying the process. I too, know that I am worth the wait, and that God makes all things new.

Confession: By Tiffany Jackson

Letting Go, Letting God. Loving God, Loving Me

Have you ever been about a mile away from a storm? You can see it in the distance, and you can smell the rain coming. You see the heavy clouds billowing in, but you're too fascinated with it to take cover. Before you know it, you're in the middle of a downpour; Soaked, cold and uncomfortable.

That's my story. It's been a while since the sky opened up above me and everything around me was flooded with a torrential down pouring of truth. I prayed the storm would relent, but it was too late for that prayer. The prayer for the moment was simply for the endurance to make it through the storm.

Just days prior, I read the following passage in Jackie Kendall's *Lady in Waiting*, ". . . When a woman stops growing spiritually, the lack of progress can often be traced back to a friendship that undermined her commitment to Jesus." I knew exactly which friendship she was referring to. The one that I refused to let go of, no matter how often I was convicted. I felt the need to compromise, in order to keep this person around. No matter how many times I had been heartbroken, and no matter how many times I walked away from him, I would return. No matter how many prayers I prayed or times I fasted, I would not let him go. I would not let the idea of 'us' go. The idea of a relationship was my 'golden calf' and I worshipped it.

Every time, I would convince myself that this relationship 'can' work; I can make it work. I can be the woman he wants me to be. I had become so detached from myself. I lived for his approval, attention and affection. I couldn't go ten minutes without thinking about him. If he communicated with me, it made my day. But if he didn't, I was flooded with a million thoughts of why he didn't or why he wasn't answering my calls or texts. The first thought was always that he was with someone else; someone prettier, smarter, funnier, and sexier. The next barrage of thoughts would highlight all of my flaws: I'm too fat, I'm ugly, I'm boring, I'm a nag, I'm not fun, I'm not good in bed, my forehead is too big, my breasts are too small, I'm a bad dancer, I'm easy, I'm a hypocrite, and on. Then I'd conclude, I can't blame him for not wanting to be with me: I'm so insecure, I'm too emotional, I'm too suspicious, I'm so annoying, I'm so desperate, I'm pathetic, he probably feels sorry for me. These voices were loud and incessant. The only way I could seem to quiet them would be to prove them wrong, by trying to contact him again. I needed him to answer. Only his response could validate me. Only he could quiet the choir of critics. But, he rarely did. I would convince myself that physical intimacy meant that there was something more there. Even if I could only keep him around through manipulation and guilt, that would have to do.

I would have moments of absolute clarity, when I knew I was being irrational and needed to let go. But those moments never lasted long. It seemed that just as I had built up the resolve to walk away, he would do something that led me to believe there was a glimmer of hope after all; a kind gesture, an invitation, a call, anything that foretold of a possible fairytale ending.

I could smell the rain of this impending storm for years. I needed to get back on track, spiritually. I needed to give myself fully to the process of shedding my false identity and fully embracing the call to mature into the woman that I knew I could be. As much as I wanted to blame him and play the role of the victim, truthfully, it was 'my choice' to stay on this course. In that moment, I decided to do what I knew I needed to do. It was time to heal the broken little girl in me, so that the woman within me could emerge.

Ironically, during this time I knew Dr. Lindsay and the Worth The Wait Revolution movement. However, rather than reaching out for help from my WTWR family, I drifted and allowed the shame and guilt to keep me bound. Once I finally reached out and opened up with my WTWR family, I didn't encounter the ridicule that I feared. There was only love and restoration. We truly overcome by the blood of the Lamb and the word of our testimony.

Confession: By Sherritta Matthews

WOW! From the first time that I heard of this Sexual Purity Revolution, I was in awe of it. How could I become apart, after being a mother of two and a long road of promiscuity? I have never been molested or raped, and all the men in my life were great family men. I had a natural dad, another dad (from mom's marriage) and God, so there were no known voids, to explain my promiscuity. I simply had a lot of DUMB days, devaluing myself!!! Finally, accepting I had nowhere else to go, I stopped running from God. I actually allowed the Word I'd been taught since I was three years old to permeate my being. Unfortunately, during all those years of just humping, I didn't realize that I still hadn't experienced the *BEST SEX OF MY LIFE*! But, the more I heard and the more I saw . . . I wanted TO DO, what the "sexual purity" people were doing.

Now, I would be really good. No dating meant, no humping around. Cool! However, for me, no dating and no humping meant, out of sight, out of mind. When I resumed dating, I didn't realize that I'd be tested in that area. I fell and I got up and so on. The enemy deceived me to think that I didn't qualify for this lifestyle, that I was not pure at all. Thoughts would bombard me: How could you impact someone? How long do you think you'll last? Well, thank God for His Word and real people LIVING IT OUT, to help encourage me to LIVE IT OUT.

This Revolution, my sister "Linds" started, has truly INSPIRED ME; a forty year old, single mother of two, never married, with a past, to know that I'm worth it. Once I aligned myself with the will of God, He then allowed my future 'Mr.' to cross my path. Now, God is propelling us into our future, so our relationship can also minister to others. It's when we commit to God and align with His will that He will "honor" us with our natural desires. Now, my 'Mr.' and I are preparing for matrimony. I can truly say that I lined up with the will of God, and now I can partake of the *BEST SEX OF MY LIFE*!

Confession: By Melanie Bonita

It all started at the age of fourteen. Yes, the tender age of fourteen was when I had my first experience with sex. To be honest with you, I really didn't know much about sex. It seemed like EVERYONE was doing it. No one had ever taught me that sex was for the institution of marriage until much later in my life. I thought I was in love with these men, or should I say, boys. I got pregnant at the age of fifteen and had my first and only child at sixteen. Even when I got marriage at the age of eighteen, I still didn't really understand the purpose of sex or marriage. I still didn't understand the difference between love and lust. I got separated from my ex-husband at nineteen, and divorced at the age twenty.

I started dating a gentleman shorting after my divorce, who later moved in with me. Marriage had greatly increased my sex drive. We had sex several times a day. Even when we broke up, (if I wasn't in a relationship) I knew I could just call him and he would come over.

When I started going to church, I started learning about what fornication was. From "No More Sheets" by Juanita Bynum, to attending a Singles Conference in North Carolina, hosted by Bishop TD Jakes, (featuring Juanita Bynum) the Lord began to change me. That night at the Singles Conference, I made a commitment not to fornicate anymore and to keep myself until I was married. Well, that lasted about a year. I was trying to do it without the help of Holy Spirit. I read books like "I Kissed Dating Goodbye" by Joshua Harris, but never sought full understanding of what I was reading. I had my own agenda.

I started dating a gentleman that I planned to bring back to church, but instead, I started having sex with him. A ministry leader spoke with us about not fornicating. Instead, I continued having sex with him. After we broke up, I was determined not to have sexual intercourse anymore. The next person I started dating was a minister, but he ALSO wanted to have sex with me. However, no matter what, I stood my ground. After we broke up, I started having a real relationship with the Lord. I started reading His word and really having a prayer life. Through prayer and an understanding of who I am, I have been able to abstain from sexual intercourse for over twelve years now. I'm not saying it has always been easy, but with God ALL things are possible. I know that because God delivered me from my sexual sin, He can deliver anyone!

Confession: By J. Lewis

As a teenager, I made the decision to wait until marriage to have sex and by God's grace, I'm still waiting today. My journey however, has not been one of perfection. In 2007, the Lord began to show me that just because I had not had sex yet, did not mean I was pure; in reality I was far from it. At the time, I was struggling to monitor my thought life, because I regularly entertained lustful thoughts fueled by the romance novels I read. As I began to seek Him more, He taught me that purity not only involved my body, but my heart and mind as well.

I set a goal to focus on learning more about purity. In a few months time, He led me to the Worth The Wait Revolution website. I read Dr. Lindsay's book, in addition to the testimonies on the site. I was tremendously encouraged to discover that I was not alone. There were other believers like me who wanted to live a pure life before the Lord. Later that year, when I saw they were having a nationwide Model Call, I knew I had to go. When I saw the WTWR models walk the runway and later share their testimonies, I was in awe and was excited about the chance to be a part of this powerful ministry. Unfortunately, I hadn't yet realized my own worth.

A short time later, I encountered a season of temptation. Even with all of my new found knowledge, I fell short when it was time for life application. I foolishly placed myself within a compromising position, thinking I could "handle it", because I did not plan on going "all the way". Before I knew it, things went further than what I intended and a pattern of sin was established in my life. During this season, God's mercy kept me. Though I didn't have sex, I learned the hard way that simply getting close to "the line" can lead to great heartache as well. In the aftermath, I partially blamed God for my hurt. I wondered why He let things get out of hand, when He knew that's not what I intended to do. He lovingly corrected me. He showed me that when we don't set out to do His will and obey Him with our whole heart, we open the door to sin and place ourselves on a path to destruction.

Through the guidance of the Holy Spirit, godly counsel from supportive friends and the example of those in WTWR, I have learned what it means to be renewed and restored. Now, at twenty-nine years of age, the wait is not easy, but truly it is His grace that is keeping me. There is a conscious effort on my part to stay connected to those that share the same standard of purity. I thank God for the

Worth The Wait Revolution and others like it that boldly uphold and proclaim God's standard!

Confession: By Kristian Harding

As a young girl purity, had always been implanted in the back of my mind due to simple morals that I had obtained without living a TRUE Christ-like life. Holding hands, rubbing, touching and kissing were all listed under MY "okay" moral standards, as long as there was no penetration. I deceived myself to think that as long as I didn't have sex or get pregnant before I graduated from high school, everything was good. Therefore, about a week after I graduated from high school, June 8, 2009, I gave up my purity to someone I thought was the love of my life and future husband. He turned out to be an ex-boyfriend of two years and that quickly moved on. There was no happy ending to this "love story".

Though I was able to at least get out of High school without fornicating, life definitely wasn't easy when it boiled down to fighting temptations. Getting through high school can be crucial if you don't know how to put your foot down when the enemy tries to send others to tempt you into sexual impurity and, "trying something new". One of my personal temptations was not just fornication, but homosexuality. I was best friends with a girl who was a pronounced lesbian. I didn't mind, because we were "just friends". We didn't have an undercover relationship going on, but it definitely wasn't the normal girly—latest fashion, boy talk—kind of friendship either. There were times when those thoughts and desires would try to overtake me, but a little piece of me always wanted to be pleasing to God. I knew His views on homosexuality, but I also knew I DID NOT WANT TO BE HOMOSEXUAL, even though the desires were there. It wasn't until I got into an AMAZING bible teaching, bible believing church that I learned how to live for Christ.

I attended my first Singles Conference at Spirit of Faith in Gainesville, Florida where I heard Dr. Lindsay Warren speak on the importance of sexual purity. I learned how the simple hugging, slight kissing, touching, humping and bumping were equivalent to penetration because of their ability to lead to sex and how it wasn't pleasing to God. After hearing this powerful lesson, fornication just wasn't the same. Yes, I tried it again, but that shortly came to an end. The Holy Spirit was there to constantly convict me of my actions, which ruined everything. Why did I continue to sin? I hadn't really caught the true revelation of how much my sin was hurting God. I wasn't ready to crucify my flesh and give God full control over my life. I knew what I wanted, but God had much more for me. I honestly had to pray for God to be my strength and to guide me. Not long after I prayed, ungodly relationships began to break off. But God didn't just leave me alone when others broke away, He sent amazing Christian friends to surround me like links creating an unbreakable chain. I learned how to overcome the enemy's tactics, and how to use my words to defeat the plans from the enemy! The good news is YOU CAN DO IT TOO!!!

Confession: By Crystal Calhoun

Growing up, I always knew that sex was to be reserved for marriage, but it wasn't until my early twenties that I realized how precious my virginity was to God. I thought you could listen to songs with sexually charged lyrics or even watch TV shows that made fornication look glamorous. As long as I wasn't having sex, those things were fine. That is not the case! God expects us to be pure, not only in our bodies, but in our thought lives as well. My passion for purity was ignited when I began to see the unfortunate consequences of those around me who participated in sex before marriage. Some were faced with unwanted pregnancies, while others experienced severe heartache from a guy who just wasn't interested in them anymore. I knew that if I was serious about my virginity, and if I wanted to follow God's plan, I had to make some serious adjustments to keep myself pure.

I surrendered to God totally one night in my room, and I began to obey His voice concerning my choice of music and television programs. When I cut out those things that could be detrimental to my purity, God began to pour more of Himself into me.

Unfortunately, I didn't know a lot of people who were committed to purity until one day when I was watching "106 and Gospel" on BET. I was so blessed to see a beautiful young woman, who was a virgin and proud of it. It was Dr. Lindsay Marsh Warren. I immediately ran to my computer and googled her name to find out all I could about "Worth The Wait Revolution". Dr. Lindsay and her ministry have truly blessed my life, I am so grateful that God led me to turn on the TV that day. When Dr. Lindsay was married, I probably was just as excited as she was. Her marriage is living proof of God's faithfulness, and I look forward to the day when I can share that same testimony with others.

Confession: By Chelsea Jean-Mary

I grew up as a Christian. However, the issue of sexual purity was always a sensitive and confusing issue for two reasons. The pressures of the world around me (high school, media, and friends) made abstinence seem out of the question. Secondly, I had no real role models around me that were living pure lives, (not just with their mouths, but with their bodies). So, I always thought that I would follow the world's way and save *it* for that 'right guy'.

Until I met this old lady:

Do you believe that God sends people in your life at the right time, for a purpose? I do. I met this woman some years ago, while I was in high school. She was a little old frail woman who identified as black, but looked white and spoke Haitian Creole even though she wasn't Haitian. She told me her life story. She used to be a doctor worked in a hospital for some years before she retired in Florida. She married her first boyfriend!!! Can you believe that? She dated one guy and that was the guy she ended up marrying!! It was quite a story now that I think about it. I was so impressed with this, black female doctor who married to the first man she dated. She encouraged me to wait on things to happen in due season.

I would love to say that I waited for my husband, but I didn't. I had to do it my way. I had my first boyfriend my freshman year of college. We broke up by the summer's end, when we realized we were going in different directions. My direction ended at the Lord's feet and his direction ended at the feet of another girl my age. I did learn my lesson though. I was able to keep my physical purity for the most part. Moreover, I was inspired to pursue the path of purity. It's a daily decision. Every morning, I have to wake up and think:

I will not pursue a guy just because I am bored.

I will not pursue a guy just because he is gorgeous.

I will use discernment to do things the right way.

Plus, on the real: I want to see how God is going to show up! He's faithful. Go purity!!!!! (Fist pump!)

<u>Confession:</u> By: Alison McMeans

Dwayne was the pizza delivery guy with prettiest eyes and shy smile that came to my Logan Circle apartment. He moved in with me two months later. At first, playing house as a grown-up was fun. It was exciting to come home to "my man." But I soon found myself ignoring the obvious signs of his growing substance abuse problem. Soon, I convinced myself that I could help him; fix him. He needed me. Deep down, maybe I thought I needed him too; to love me so much that it filled in the cracks of my soul; cracks created from the constant insults for being so tall and so fat; crack created from my glasses, my bad perm, my braces. The emptiness started at age eleven. My father died at home in front of me, due to a heart attack. I thought by giving everything I had, (my money, my attention, my body), maybe he'd think I was good enough to be loved. But no matter how much I gave, neither one of us could love each other enough to fill those empty places within. My apartment was quickly deteriorating due to the damage he'd caused while being drunk and high. I'd clean him, clean the mess and put him to bed. He stole from me. He stole from my friends. After he lost his job, I worked extra hours to pay back what he took and to make ends meet. I dodged my closest friends. In guilt and shame, I turned away from my friends, and turned away from God. Then, he cheated on me; brought his ex-girlfriend into my home while I was away. Thankfully, my anger was stronger than my fear of being alone, and I put him out of the house and my life.

Months later, I met Todd and was instantly taken by his hundred watt smile and witty conversation. He didn't drink or smoke. He had a good job, drove a nice car and had his own place. I hoped he'd be worthy of receiving everything I had to give and immediately got to work on making him love me. Then one night, he answered his cell phone and began an illicit conversation with the woman on the other end, as he lay in bed with me. Unfortunately, I found myself in a place I seemed to come back to, over and over again. I blamed these men and the others before them for my pain. Why couldn't someone love me? Why did I always give my all and just receive *'hurt'* in return. But then, something clicked. These men were treating me this way, because I had let them. I had freely given my heart and my body to them without condition, without expectation, without commitment. Being with them meant I had to stifle that voice inside that told me these relationships and the things we did were wrong. I'd forgotten that I was a "fearfully and wonderfully made" creation of God and should be cared for as such. My feelings and desires weren't the issue; it was my mishandling them. Sex is a gift from God. Our bodies are a gift from God. When I finally realized that I needed to honor the sacredness of my body and the spirit that lives within it, my eyes were opened.

With brand new clarity and understanding, I decided to stop this cycle until I found the right man; my husband. I wanted to enjoy the pleasures of sex without the feelings that would always follow: the guilt, the regret, the shame. I wanted to be so in tuned with the voice of God that I couldn't miss a word. I wanted to use my body, as well as my voice to praise and honor my Creator.

It's been years since I made the decision to wait and this journey has not always been a smooth one. Sometimes I wish that whenever I was in a situation that wasn't quite "within the will of God," I could recall a scripture, take a deep breath and instantly escape the temptation. However, faith is no magic trick and God is not a 'genie in a bottle'. I have strong, unshakable faith, but struggle with my desires. I love God and hate when I do things that are not pleasing to him. I go to church, enjoy praise and worship, and still have to check a thought or two, about a good looking man in the congregation. (Hey, I'm a work in progress!) But every day I make the decision to control my thoughts and behavior. I didn't choose to wait out of bitterness, or anger and I don't feel like I'm being deprived or missing out on something. This time has allowed me to strengthen my relationship with God and see my true worth. I refuse to be overlooked or under-loved any longer. I realize that God's plan is to keep my heart protected until I meet someone who truly loves and values me.

Confession: By Bola Shittu

My Sex Life, My Spiritual Life and My Body as the Temple Of God

At the age of thirteen, I started my menstrual period. My mother told me that because I started menstruating, I could get pregnant at anytime. Therefore, she said, I should not go near boys. As the thought of getting pregnant scared the living daylight out of me, I steered clear of boys. However, some of my friends were already having sex and they told too many stories of their escapades. Wanting to feel the way they were feeling, but not wanting to indulge in the actual act of sex, I developed the habit of daydreaming, watching and reading pornography. I had unending sex in my mind with multiple men, just like the women in movies. Porn even improved my gym life, because I could run all day long on the treadmill reading a good porn story. My mind was consumed with demonic thoughts. Now that I am a Christian, I realize that the battleground is the mind.

After eventually having real sex, I was still intoxicated with watching and reading porn. I longed to have unending sex with random partners, like in the books and movies, but I was not bold enough to carry it out. When I got married, I was a faithful wife, having enough good sex, but the day dreaming ad pornography didn't stop. My addiction was fueled, because I could not reach an orgasm with my husband. Eventually, a coworker introduced me to sex toys and the first time I used one, it gave me pleasures I had never experienced with any man, pleasures I never thought possible. Hence, another destructive hobby took place in my life.

To the glory of God, I rededicated myself back to Him two years ago. Little by little, I started renewing my mind, cleansing it with the blood of Jesus, and asking God to help me with my addiction to pornography.

If I wrote that the process was easy, I'd be lying. If I wrote that through the healing and cleansing period, I wasn't tempted to use sex toys, read/watch porn, I'd be lying. If I wrote that I didn't struggle more than once, I'd be lying again and again. Each time I fell, I got up again. Now, glory to God, the addiction is gone. Scriptures like 1 Corinthians 6:19-20, really helped me. It states,

'Do you not know that your bodies are temples of the Holy Spirit, who is in you, whom you have received from God? You are not your own; you were bought at a price. Therefore honor God with your bodies".

Pornography took my focus off of the things of God and attempted to destroy and delay my destiny. However, God's mercy prevailed and, I have been healed. I have abstained with the help of God.

Zechariah 4:6 says ". . . *not by might, nor by power, but by My Spirit, says the Lord of Host"*. With God's help, I have conquered and overcome the stronghold of pornography. I rededicated my life back to God and I have become a born-again virgin. When I remarry, we will wait for that special night to have the best sex of our lives, because I believe more than ever that I am worth the wait.

Confession: By Mariama Whyte

When Dr. Warren, whom I affectionately call "Lins", asked me to share my story, I immediately said yes simply because I truly respect Lindsay and the unique ministry God has given her. We've known each other since our teenage years in high school, played sports together, share mutual friends, eventually became sisters in Christ and continue to support each other's endeavors. And recently, it was such a blessing for me to witness and celebrate in her joy as a beautiful new bride to her husband, Gareth, at their wedding. Although it was easy for me to say yes to her request, it is not as easy to articulate my journey for it hasn't been the smoothest of roads. And as I write, I'm going through the phases of my life, digging to find the root of some of the insecurities that stayed with me for years and that I sometimes struggle with today.

All of us have a moment when we became conscious of the significance of our sexual identity. It's different for everyone, but for me I remember when I was in the 2nd grade as a new student in a new school system, feeling somewhat different and isolated because I had to make new friends as well as go through a special reading program to perform at the same level as the other kids in my class. That special program did wonders for my confidence academically, but that same year I received a lot of attention from a few boys who would chase me home every day while they were taunting me, sometimes using profanities, and touching me inappropriately. Fortunately my big sister, Miata, was there to knock them upside the head with her lunch box to keep them away from her little sister. To some, this may seem like innocent child's play, but for me it wasn't. Eventually, these boys were suspended for their behavior and they never messed with me again. But the seed was planted and the idea that my body was the source of enjoyment and even boyish ridicule messed with me for years. As I grew up, if I was approached by someone, I would always wonder, "Does he like me for me or does he just want my body?" And without the patience to find out the answer, I'd find myself "giving it up." I was always questioning whether being me was enough. Whether my 2nd grade experience or being raised without my father's physical presence in my home, or peer pressure, or just simply being influenced by the culture in which we live fed my insecurity, it stayed with me for years. And while I excelled in my academics, developed my talents through music, performances, sports and eventually my professional career, I was insecure.

Even as I accepted Christ into my heart, as a teenager and a young woman, I experienced a lot of what some would call mistakes and misfortunes; losing my virginity at fourteen, abortions, date rape, and eventually moving from one relationship to the next without any plan of healing in between. As a young woman, I used to beat myself up for being so careless. But as I matured, I began to embrace the lessons from those experiences and have since forgiven myself for being a kid who really didn't know any better and have forgiven those who hurt me. In fact, many of my relationships were quite positive. But when I began to understand my own value, things began to change for me. As a young girl, I didn't give much thought to the beauty and value of my body, nor did I give much thought to marriage. I didn't grow up dreaming about my wedding day, so the idea of saving my virginity until marriage was irrelevant. Actually, I was daydreaming about performing and writing.

Other than my grandparents who were married for sixty-two years, I didn't see many examples of long-term relationships. I had no real conversations or lessons on sex or what makes for a successful, lasting union. My mother encouraged us to wait until we were physically and emotionally mature enough to handle our bodies. My father would tell us the importance of remaining virgins until we got married. But it didn't quite stick. I was intrigued by the idea of waiting, but after having girl-talk with my high school friends who encouraged me to "try it," my curiosity got the best of me. After all, I was the last virgin in the group and the boy I was dating was ca-yute! So once I started having sex, the thought of stopping AND waiting until marriage was not at the top of my "to-do list". To be real, sex feels good and it feels great with someone that you really care about. But through my late 20's into my 30's, I realized that I wanted more from my relationships than what I allowed myself to experience. I wanted more than to give all of myself away, calling someone my boyfriend for a few years only to eventually break up and go through the same cycle again with someone else. Through the years, I always heard God's voice speaking to me, "slow down", "wait," "now's not the time," "he's not the one," "I love you." And at times, I've listened and obeyed. And for several months, I would remain abstinent. But just as I was disciplined in eating well, getting to my rehearsals on time, or knocking them out in my auditions to land a gig, my abstinence was also a means to end. As soon as someone would come along and half way sweep me off my feet, that was enough to open myself up to him without any semblance of commitment. But that's not enough anymore.

What I want now more than anything is experiencing real, unconditional love; a connection with God, with a man, and with myself. That sounds so cliché and we've heard it over and over again. "You can't love someone until you love yourself." But it's so true. Until you know you're priceless, you'll always give yourself away too easily. Until you really understand and honor God's Spirit within you, you'll treat your body cheaply with no regard to the consequences; Sometimes deadly consequences. It's taken me years to get to this place of self-realization and surrender in God. It took single motherhood to my son, Micaiah, for me to finally sit still and learn patience, acceptance and to better define what I want and need in my life. It took time away from my career and more devoted time to my own emotional development to appreciate my alone time and the innocence of laughter and friendship "without benefits." It's refreshing to have this new sense of freedom and contentment.

So my choice to reclaim my purity is not just with my body, but also with my heart and my mind. It's a choice born out of brokenness and fueled by my desire to be whole. That's the best gift I can give to myself and to anyone else. I've cried some big tears, but I'm so happy to say I'm healed from my past, I'm content with where I am and excited for the future. My dreams have definitely expanded outside of performing and writing. I will admit that every now and then I dream of my wedding day. It's a beautiful thought ☺ But more than that, I dream and pray for the success of my marriage with the man I choose to love, respect, and honor. I pray that I can receive his love purely and give it in the same way. And if it took years of good and not so good experiences for me to come to this new place of peace where he can find me pure and whole, then it was all worth it.

Confession: By Michelle Thomas

As I look back on my connection with Worth The Wait Revolution, I understand that this divine connection was in God's heart even before I knew it existed. I knew nothing about this ministry. I hadn't seen any media clips, runway shows, nor encountered any of the WTWR models. I prayed for a mentor; someone that heard HIS voice, someone that would love me with AGAPE love, someone with a pure heart. In 2006 those prayers came to pass and I was led to approach Dr. Lindsay about my desire to be mentored. At that moment, I can honestly say that my life began to change in a great way. Worth The

Wait Revolution has challenged my life beyond measure. The fruit has resulted in so many unexplainable ways.

During a season of brokenness, I experienced an enormous amount of chaos in unhealthy relationships. These trying experiences resulted in emotional, verbal, and sometimes physical abuse. I longed for the chaos to cease. I needed a change. I needed peace. The prayers and the connection to WTWR provided me with another focus; a more positive focus. I am so appreciative of HIS GRACE and POWER because HE made that connection a reality for me. Consequently, my entire household will never be the same. Now, I walk in whole life prosperity and my beautiful daughter walks in whole life prosperity. By making an executive decision to live out His Word, rest in HIM, cast my CARE upon HIM, and SEEK HIM for instructions, the Lord has keep me. Through WTWR, and my connection to Dr. Lindsay, I have learned successful tools that I consistently use in new and unchartered territory.

Confession: By Yaida Oni Ford

I promised God at the age of sixteen that I would remain a virgin until marriage. Unknowingly, I would have incredible challenges keeping the promise. I had never heard of sexual purity, and did not know God's Word when I made the promise. I knew I struggled with forms of sexual perversion but did not know where it came from. I felt like a deviant and never said a word to anyone about it. Later I learned about generational curses and addictions that become strongholds in our homes and affect our children. As I read God's Word, then I understood that God has given us the authority to live a pure life, in Christ Jesus. I wanted to remain pure.

But then, more hurdles came during my adulthood. I frequently had married men, including pastors and preachers, approaching me inappropriately. It almost destroyed me because I did not understand why God would allow these situations to come in my life when I was trying to walk uprightly. I was barely holding on, when God sent the right people into my life to help me heal in those areas. I also discovered Worth The Wait Revolution along the way. I realized I was not the only one dealing with and healing from this hurt. God had not forsaken me.

Now, I have amazing, pure relationships with genuine men of God. I encourage other women to befriend men as their brothers so they can truly get to know them without the distractions of lust, misguided notions and deception. I am living proof that it is possible to have healthy, godly relationships with the opposite sex, regardless of whether you have been the predator or the prey. Just allow God to heal you and choose to view others with "His eyes".

Confession: By Roberta James

When I was maybe about ten or eleven, I remember being left alone at home in the care of my uncles. As they were sound asleep, I woke up, struggling to get one of my cousins off of me. He tried and tried to have sex with me, but I fought as hard as I could. No penetration. I was too afraid and embarrassed to share this with any family member. To this very day, nobody even knows. I think I feared more for his life than mine.

In my teenager years, my stepfather would make his way into my bedroom, but I would fight again for my virginity. It got to the point that I had to lock my bedroom door at night or push the dresser to keep him out. One day, I got tired of living in fear so I told my mom. Her heart was broken, but she didn't leave him. Then, he found his next victim, my sister. We have both forgiven my mom and our stepdad. I've learned that people do things that were once done to them.

Throughout my teenage years, I would begin to crave sex and I didn't know why. I think it resulted from that single act of my cousin trying to force himself on me. I did some crazy things like masturbation and some other ungodly acts. Could an instance of molestation and attempted rape lead to a life of promiscuity? I was so naive to believe that the very men I slept with loved me, for me. They only desired one thing.

I've asked God to forgive me and cleanse me from all of the impurities I had in my life. I'm very cautious about what I watch on TV or hear on the radio. I've limited conversations with certain friends who I know are living opposite of what I'm trying to live. There is no need to hang around someone who will try to influence me to go back to doing what I know is displeasing to God.

Well, I can say that I've been living a life of purity for over one year and I have never felt so good in my life. It is hard sometimes, no lie. Most importantly, what keeps me strong is my relationship with Christ. I realize that my body is not mine to give away to anybody, not even myself. Now, I treasure my singleness as a gift to God. As a single, I feel that it my duty to be a positive role model for my son.

Thank God for all my mentors who have written books on sexual purity such as Juanita Bynum, Ty Adams and my dear friend Lindsay Warren. God has truly placed these three women on my path to sexual purity.

Confession: By Taneeka Strickland

My sexual purity journey began at an early age although I never really called it that . . .

My Parents' taught me to "wait until you are married to have sex" since I was around seven years old. I didn't think much about it at the time because I was only seven and I really wasn't even interested in liking anybody let alone anything else. Of course, as I got older, I became interested in boys. I did like a few people, but I was already paying attention to how the boys treated the 'fast' girls, who they frequently talked about after getting whatever it was they wanted from them. I had no interest in becoming the subject of those conversations, nor was I the least bit comfortable with the rumors that were associated with the girls who had already developed a reputation. I decided pretty independently that I wanted to meet a boy that would respect me and value me and that I was willing to wait to have a boyfriend until I met that person. So, although I was pure all the way through middle and high school it really wasn't about my relationship with God at the time, it was more about self-respect.

In college, my motivation became more about standing out, being proud to be considered "a good girl". I was proud of myself for being one of a few virgins left and that no matter what, I could be assured that anyone that liked me, REALLY liked me for me. I set major boundaries with any guy I spent time with because I wanted him to know that being with me would be different, and the ones that couldn't get with my boundaries made it easy for me to identify what they were really about. Plus, I decided that whoever I married would be incredibly special (and not to mention FINE) and that he would take pride in knowing that *I waited just for him*. As time went on I began pursuing a relationship with God more and more, but still partying and doing 'my thing'. As I got closer to God, I saw the value that my virginity had in pleasing Him. In my heart, I solidified that even if I did nothing else, I would please God by staying a virgin until I got married.

After I graduated, that's when the journey REALLY began. I had just joined Spirit of Faith Christian Center where I was really being taught who I was, and how to develop a true relationship with God. I became more deeply inspired to serve God with my lifestyle. My journey became harder at this point though, because I met and dated some guys that I actually really liked and my desire to have sex was a lot stronger. As I got older, I wanted to get married and being "a good girl" was no longer enough. I became more and more impatient that I had yet to meet *the one*. By the age of twenty-eight, I had already purchased a home, acquired a good job, lived a holy lifestyle and I was also serving at church. I attended all of the Singles events and did everything I felt I was to do, and yet, I still wasn't married.

I became frustrated. I felt that my friends could no longer relate to me, as they were all married or were in serious relationships. I was a bridesmaid more times than I can remember and I was ready for the wait to be over. As I gained more dating experience, it became harder and harder to wait. I was tired of being on that journey alone; I needed to find someone who could understand where I was. Thank God, I found out about Worth The Wait Revolution. Joining Worth the Wait Revolution was the source of true support and motivation that I was looking for. As a person that still likes to look nice and have fun, I sought out others who were still "fly enough to wait". I have learned that being content is a process and I have grown a lot along the way. Dr. Lindsay, is definitely FLY, and has been the source of motivation that dreams do come true; as I have watched her walk the wait out over the years until being married to her very own Prince Charming.

As my wait continues as a virgin at thirty-four years old, I have stayed true to my commitment to my Parents', myself, and most importantly to God. Although there have been some major close calls, and major heartbreak, my journey continues and I plan to finish strong. As a matter of fact, my future Husband will actually be reading my testimony in this book one day and MY wait will be complete! Here's to the journey . . . . !

Confession: By Canden Webb

I can't remember a time in my life where I wasn't being attacked sexually. From the time I was a little girl and was exposed to porn and dirty magazines, through grossly inappropriate touches from an elderly man at the age of eight, being groped by a trusted family friend at an auto shop, or being introduced to lesbianism during sleep-overs with one of my girl cousins; I've pretty much been exposed to it all. Satan was determined to destroy my purity but God had so much more planned for me. Raised in the church and knowing better, I refused to be bound to the lust that was present all around me growing up. I couldn't let Satan tell me who I was. I had to believe what the bible said about me in order to survive. Even when I lost my virginity at the age of twenty-four to the guy who I was dating on and off at the time, God still used it for His glory to show me how relaxed I had become in my spirituality and restored my heart back to Him. Today, I am twenty-eight years old and have remained abstinent for four years. When I met my Worth The Wait Revolution family I was right at home. Every day is a testimony for the great life I am destined for. I am so grateful for God's love covering me each night with reminders that I AM and have always been WORTH THE WAIT.

Confession: By Jessica Tolbert

Me? A pregnant teen? By my own father? No way! I could recall at least two pregnancy scares when I missed my period. I sat in the bathroom, pleading with God: *Lord, no! This can't happen! I have my whole life ahead of me!* Fourteen years—that's how long the cycle of sexual abuse lasted. From eight to twenty-two, that part of my private life was kept in the dark, masked by my sweet personality, bright smile, and personal accomplishments that most people knew best about me. At such a young age, I was oblivious to the impact of my dad touching me like that for the first time, which eventually escalated into manual stimulation, oral sex, and intercourse (never with protection). He manipulated me to keep me from exposing him, and for a long time, it worked. I was a "Daddy's girl." Wasn't I supposed to be able to trust him? I didn't think anyone would understand and I didn't want to be rejected, so I kept it all to myself. Years had gone by, but my silence of "being alone" was tearing me up inside. Confused. Ashamed. Desperate. Alone. Weary. I often contemplated suicide (but never attempted it). Life wasn't worth living if it meant continuing in this seemingly never-ending cycle. At thirteen, I accepted Jesus Christ into my life. But as a young Christian caught in the middle of that mess, I struggled not just emotionally, physically, and mentally, but also spiritually like never before. It seemed like there was no light at the end of the tunnel, but I still held onto the hope that God would make a breakthrough.

My relationship with my dad continued to spiral downward as he began to verbally and physically abuse me when I refused to satisfy him sexually. Fueled by anger to the point where he was no longer the father I once knew, he accused me of being a lesbian because I wouldn't give in to his sexual advances. He even perverted Scripture to justify his actions. His words cut me deeply, planting negative seeds into my life. He threatened to leave the family if I didn't comply, argued that I didn't love him, and tried to convince me that my mom gave him consent to continue in his incest. To make it worse, my mother was distant from me. I yearned for that mother-daughter bond. I just wanted her to hug me and to hear her say, "I love you." Her selfishness, apathy, and detachment hurt me just as much as the abuse from my dad. Sadly, the one whose love and affection I needed (my mom), rarely ever showed it, and the one who did show me love and affection, abused it (my dad).

Due to the struggles I faced at home, I later got involved in a friendship with a girl that crossed boundaries over time. She made advances toward me and I reluctantly welcomed them. It was an undercover toxic relationship. I quenched the Holy Spirit while keeping up the good Christian façade. Yet the Spirit convicted me of my rebelliousness and audacity to turn my back on God. I finally saw through the deception that Satan so carefully crafted to be alluring. I was a hypocrite, showing myself to be "holy" in the eyes of others, while growing colder toward God and diving deeper into my sinful ways. But in God's love and mercy, He met me where I was at and remained faithful even when I wasn't. In August 2009, I came to the end of myself. I was tired of being tired. I didn't want to lead my own life anymore. I just wanted God to take full control so that I could live a life pleasing to Him.

On my knees I prayed, asking God to forgive me of every sin I could possibly remember committing. I told Him exactly how I felt—miserable, lost, drained, remorseful, afraid—and asked that He remove my guilt and shame, cleanse me from the inside out, change my heart and mind, and keep me from falling away again. In faith, I fully surrendered *everything* to Him. At that moment, a huge burden was lifted off of me, and I felt the kind of peace that surpasses all understanding. I knew Jesus as my Savior, but up until now, I hadn't allowed Him to reign as *Lord* over my life.

As a consequence of his sin, my dad is no longer in my life. In God's perfect timing, I was led to open up to a friend named

Omar, who spent countless hours comforting, encouraging, and challenging me to seek God during this time. I also received Christian counseling, which played a significant role in my healing process. As of August 27, 2011, I can happily and thankfully say that not only is Omar my best friend and confidant, he is also my husband and "my other whole." Never in my life did I think that I could receive such a blessing, someone who loves me unconditionally the way God does. Although Omar and I have had our share of struggles to remain pure before marriage, God graciously kept us for each other. My purity had been selfishly stripped away by my father, but in Christ I'm a "born-again virgin." There is hope and victory in Jesus! I am an overcomer. God has fully restored, renewed, redeemed, and transformed my life. He truly delivered me. And He can do that for you too!

Confession: By Tomeka B. Scales

I was never considered cool or popular. I was recognized . . . as the girl who probably knows the answers to the test or the girl who would make a good study partner. Academically, I was excelling, but socially, not so much. I was introverted and many considered me "antisocial." I considered myself antisocial because at times I felt insignificant. Only feeling needed when somebody wanted something can do that. If this was the case with casual friendships and associates, it was double the case for relationships. I might as well have been Casper because invisible, I was! How did that routine go? Oh yeah, I like you, you pay no attention to me, and you date someone else. Figures! But wouldn't I be a catch? Intelligent, caring, most importantly a woman of God who values her relationship with the Most High and is not ashamed to proclaim it! Well, in a world that praises and awards debauchery, these qualities made me boring. It's okay I told myself. I will not curse, I will not smoke, and I will wait until marriage to have sex. The feelings of inadequacy started to get the best of me. I just knew if the right guy came along, I could prove I was great! Isn't it funny how you can convince yourself of becoming great when greatness already lives within? A guy came along; I was so sure that he was "The One" that I would have done anything for him. Didn't matter that he really was everything I didn't want. Really? Was I going to settle for someone who smoked weed and talked freely to me about his sex-scapades when I knew those were not a qualities I was interested in. Yep, I was! Whatever he wanted me to do, I probably would have done. I wanted so badly to get him that I shared my feelings and of course he threw my heart onto the train tracks in front of which we were standing. After my shock of complete rejection wore off, I became extremely depressed. Not just because of my feelings of inadequacy being compounded, but I felt guilty for feeling this way when there were people all around the world going through much more painful experiences. Who am I to cry over a boy who does not even want me? But, it was what it was and I had to move on. Slowly, but surely I did. I have now realized that my past experiences shaped who I am. As Donald Lawrence sings, "the best is yet to come." At the age of twenty-seven, I still do not curse, smoke, and continue to save myself for the guy that is perfect for me. I will not settle for less. As Dr. Warren says in the book, *The Best Sex of My Life*, your heart is the birthplace for your dreams, desires, and destiny, and guarding your heart means guarding your destiny. I actively choose on a daily basis to guard my destiny. I will lead by example and continue to show that being "cool" or "popular" means nothing if you cannot respect yourself enough to feel worthy of God's best.

Confessions of a Sexual Purity Revolution, Part II

The Gentlemen

And they have overcome (conquered) him by means
of the blood of the Lamb and by the utterance of their testimony . . .
Revelation 12:11a

Confession: By Steven Keith

My mother was a single parent of five children. My parents divorced while I was very young. After the divorce, she moved back to her Mississippi home with her children. My father lived in another state so my older brothers became my role models. Despite growing up in a Southern Baptist church, I knew very little about my purpose for going to church every service. I eventually lost my virginity in my senior year of high school. I knew little about sex prior to that. When engaging in conversations with my brothers about women, they would school me on how to wear condoms during sex. I remember catching my brothers watch pornography. There were even occasions during my teenage years, when my mom would bring bags of condoms to me, from the local Health Department, just as a precaution. Since I don't recall sex being a hot topic in church, I was totally unaware of its purpose, other than having a little fun and making babies.

The first year of my Air Force career was an experience. I found a church and learned more information in one year, than in the previous nineteen years of attending the former Baptist church. I had given my life to God and was a faithful member. However, past choices began to take root and within four and a half years of walking with Christ, I backslid. Then, I covered it up. The only one who knew was God. Unfortunately, my flesh went on a rampage. I escalated from setting up harmless dating profiles, to looking at explicit pictures of women on the sites, to purchasing pornography; and eventually, soliciting dirty phone and internet conversations. While all this took place, I still served faithfully in my church. While at my new duty location, I entered my first relationship, which I kept very private. We did everything one could imagine. The behavior continued long enough, that I lost sight of God's plan for me. Even though our relationship ended, my sexual appetite and addictions followed me through my next three duty stations. By the time I moved to the D.C. metro area, I was way out of control.

Despite the many convictions, it seemed nearly impossible to find strength to get my life together. I was hurt from my past. I realized that I had taken on my father's addiction to women. One day, I walked into Spirit of Faith Christian Center, heard the Word, and took that bold walk to the altar. I remember, I was so sorry for my behavior. I set my heart to change my lifestyle. I walked in purity for the next seven months and that's when I met my beautiful wife. We remained abstinent until marriage, as our walk with Christ increased. We attended a Worth The Wait Revolution Gala which sparked our interest to join the Revolution. Now that we are married, we set ourselves to use our experience to witness to couples struggling with sexual purity. God blessed our union because we were obedient to His Word. Philippians 4:13 says, "I can do all things through Christ Who strengths me." This is confirmation that our 'impossible', is possible with God!

Confession: By Omar Savory

Worth The Wait Revolution has been a tremendous blessing in my life and walk of sexual purity. Before my life in Christ, I had no desire for sexual purity and abstinence. In my early young adult life, I thought casual sex was my God given right. I had sexual encounters with women and never thought it was right or wrong. I even went as far as creating "sex goals" for myself; trying to have sex with women in each sorority, feeling that was something to accomplish as a Kappa man. I even had scares of unwanted pregnancies and diseases. Then the day came when God entered my life and changed my whole perspective. He showed me that sex was a gift and His way was the only way to enjoy it. He opened my eyes to my selfish and reckless ways. I was convicted by my actions and finally realized that the only way to live was by His rules and His ways.

When I moved to Maryland from the New York/New Jersey area, I possessed a need for godly encouragement. God met my needs by leading me to Worth The Wait Revolution. I thank God for Dr. Lindsay's obedience and bringing this Revolution forward. The encouragement from the WTWR has even been a blessing to my new marriage. I now declare that, YOU, are worth the wait.

Confession: By Davon Johnson

The door was left unlocked, and I accidently walked in on my mom having sex. From one traumatic experience to the next, one weekend, I was fondled in a dark room during a round of *Truth or Dare* by my best friend's oldest sister. Soon after, I discovered a *Playboy* magazine while snooping around someone else's house. I later began to emulate these experiences through "dry-humping," playing "doctor" and by playing "house" with other kids from my neighborhood. I became sexually active before the end of fifth grade.

After being introduced to cinematic porn and masturbation in middle school, I quickly picked up on another horrible addiction. I would sneak into my parent's bedroom at night while they were asleep to borrow their VHS tapes and DVDs, watch them in my room, and return them before they woke up. Searching for more, I turned to the internet.

With unlimited access to the World Wide Web, I went from watching heterosexual porn to watching all variations of porn. Porn became my sexual junk food—my fantasy world. They did things I was unwilling to do. So I decided to just watch and imagine as if I was one of the stars on the set. Masturbation became my only known method for practicing safe sex.

Throughout my teen years, I was seduced by several different guys to commit sexual acts with them. I was hesitant, extremely uncomfortable and told them no at first, but because I felt hopelessly peer pressured, I wanted to be accepted, and because of my own bi-curiosity, I eventually gave in to their requests. Each one of them promised that I wouldn't have to do anything—that they would do all the work.

Reality dating shows on MTV such as *Tila Tequila's Shot at Love* and gay episodes of *Next!* had me more inquisitive about the bisexual lifestyle. I wasn't *GAY* though; at least that's what I told myself. I was so afraid of being labeled, burdened with the shame of my indecent acts, too prideful to allow my reputation to be tarnished, that I would never profess with my mouth that I was gay, bi, or even D.L. To get questioning people off of my back, to protect my masculinity and to silence the convictions in my heart, I always classified myself as "straight". It wasn't really about my orientation. It was only about my gratification. Whether male or female, I just wanted to be with somebody: anyone who I could develop chemistry with, anyone who could satisfy me for that moment and who would fulfill that utterly dark void in my heart. I learned that when you are controlled by your sinful nature, there is no level of perversion or wickedness that is too great. Lust is never satisfied.

I didn't plan on getting saved, while attending college in the fall of 2008. I didn't want to give up the things that gave me pleasure. I didn't want to confirm my convictions by reading what the Bible had to say about it. I didn't want to be held accountable for the knowledge of the truth. But eventually, God's unconditional love came knocking at the door of my heart, and I could no longer lock him out. At age eighteen, I died to myself and surrendered my life to Jesus. And that utterly dark void I had in my heart—Christ filled it. Testimonies of ex-homosexuals really encouraged me to seek deliverance from the lifestyle I was in. The Pink Cross Foundation helped me to overcome my addiction to pornography.

Now at 22, God has given me a renewed mind toward sin. I'm learning to hate what he hates and to love what he loves. Temptation is still all around me, but now I desire to remain faithful to the one who has died for my sins and saved my soul from self-demoralization and eternal damnation. God has since given me a beautiful fiancée. She accepts my past as well as my new life in Christ, which is a powerful testimony. I've crossed over from darkness into light, and I've forsaken my perversions for purity. I'm glad that accepting the truth of God's Word has set me free from my bondage and has set me on the straight and narrow path to fulfill my God-ordained purpose!

Confession: By Robert Adams III

Peer pressure, music, media, and social networking sites all have one thing in common: influence. Depending on how you use them, each of these can influence your behavior positively or negatively.

As for me, it was music and media that influenced me the most. I grew up watching 106 & Park, Rap City, and other shows, attempting to identify with those who I thought were successful. I viewed their examples collectively, as the definition of a real man; Making money, chasing women, and partying. Now, I grew up in a home with a God-fearing mother who instilled in me the power of faith, but I did not want to live for Christ because I thought it would be boring and legalistic.

I watched church goers look one way in service and live another way outside of service. It became unappealing to me and I ran from Christ. I went off to college and did what I thought I should do: study hard and party harder. I was living a life with no direction, travelling on an unfamiliar road with no GPS. God was able to reach me and began to transform my thinking. Subsequently, my life changed. I encourage you to find out what God's plan of destiny is for your life. Following Christ is not a call to boredom or legalism, but a call to fulfillment.

Worth The Wait Revolution is a blessing to me. I have built relationships with a collection of people who follow Christ but still know how to have fun. For this reason, Worth The Wait Revolution makes a lasting impression on the hearts of those in the community.

"The purpose of life is a life of purpose"—Robert Byrne

Confession: By Marquis C. Brantley

In 2006, I got my hands on a copy of *"The Best Sex of My Life: a Guide to Purity"*, after attending a youth conference. To be quite frank, I was NOT interested in reading it.

So, I started reading this book, right and it really played a major role in changing my life.

I had already made a pledge to God that I would stop fornicating, but my motives behind that decision were the wrong motives. My fear of children out of wedlock and STDs caused me to say, "Okay God, I'm done with sex until I get married." However, because my decision to abstain from sex until marriage was based on *fear*, the pledge I made to God crumbled when temptation made a pass at me.

Dr. Lindsay's "Guide To Purity" taught me about true integrity below the belt. It taught me that I was WORTH waiting for. It taught me that love for God, *not fear*, should have been my motive behind the decision to honor God with my body. Being equipped with a new revelation of sexual purity, I was ready for a new level of dedication to the pledge I'd made to God.

Meanwhile, I also found myself seriously searching for a wife. I mean . . . I was in hot pursuit of this chic. I had absolutely NO idea who or where she was, but I knew she was exactly who I wanted and needed her to be. I was confident about this because I knew what I was petitioning God for.

Along with this new revelation from Dr. Lindsay, I also heard a teaching from Pastor Mike Freeman (who was not my pastor at the time), which gave me instructions on how to attract what I wanted in life. I began to apply these teachings to my life. After about three years, I began to see manifestation. My new lifestyle prompted my friend to introduce me to a friend of hers, who possessed the same values. At the time of our introduction, this new young lady happened to live 1,100 miles away in another state. But now, just under three years later, we live happily together as husband and wife (wink).

I attracted the woman I wanted in my life, but it began with my solemn promise to God to live a holy and righteous lifestyle.

Confession: By Stedman Sirmons

In the spring of 2009, I finished my sophomore year at University of Florida. After receiving disappointing grades, I was just ready to have fun and get my mind off of school. I contacted one of my best friends that I had known since middle school. He was shocked when I told him about my situation with females.

"How could a guy who looks as good as you not be smashing a different girl every other week?!!" he asked. Well, I was a nineteen year old virgin. When we were in high school, I didn't know any girls worth having sex with. (They were trashy, not classy). He was looking for quantity, I was looking for quality. I wanted a real relationship. Sex didn't matter anyway, because I had been masturbating since the seventh grade.

I decided we needed to party by the end of the week. After arriving at this party, I was offered some weed. Then I started drinking. I had about seventeen shots of liquor within an hour. That's when I met a girl who was everything I lusted after. She was a very attractive. During our conversation, I talked to her about never having a girlfriend and still being a virgin. Later on, she took me to the back room of the house. She started to get undressed. I continued kissing and doing whatever I had seen on TV, movies and porn. She asked, "are you really a virgin? You definitely seem to know what you are doing." She was pushing my head lower and lower . . . signaling for oral sex. Since neither of was completely naked, I hadn't put on a condom yet. The moment I put the condom on, I heard a voice in my head that was so loud. It sounded like someone was yelling at me. That voice was the Holy Spirit. The voice said "YOU DON'T LOVE HER!! She is NOT your wife. You don't even know her. Do you really want to have to tell your wife that you lost your virginity in a one night stand? And what about when you have kids?" I was shaken. In that moment, someone knocked on the door, and interrupted us. I pulled up my pants and left. That situation was life-changing. That was then.

Now, it is 2012. I don't drink, smoke, or masturbate. I've been transformed. I would never consider being in bed with a woman that isn't my wife. I rededicated my life back to Christ. I'm still a virgin. I've decided to wait until I'm married and do it God's way. I thank and appreciate my pastors, Kenneth and Tabatha Claytor, of Spirit of Faith Christian Center Gainesville, for challenging me to grow. I also would like to thank Lindsay Warren and her husband, Gareth Warren for inspiring me and showing me that sex is truly worth the wait.

Confession: By Jaron Rice

I have a confession. I was an addict; a junkie. But, my high didn't come from smoking something, or sticking needles in my arm. It was, however, still killing me. I was addicted to porn. I was addicted to masturbating. I was addicted to sex. I was addicted to just about anything indulgent. Lust used to cover me like a wet blanket, and was influencing every decision of my life.

As a child, I was molested by a couple of babysitters. Though the experiences were not welcomed or consensual, they did awaken sexual desires within me at far too early of an age. By the time I was ten, I was watching porn and masturbating regularly. My first consensual sexual experiences were fueled by homosexual curiosity and were carried out with my childhood best friend. I didn't consider myself gay. I wasn't physically or emotional attracted to other boys. Women were definitely my first choice, but my molestation left me scarred and naturally distrusting of women, so I directed my sexual desires towards the alternative. In fact, my friend and I used to watch heterosexual porn during homosexual experimentation. It was like drinking beer. What I mean is that, it was an acquired taste. Initially, it was disgusting, but each time it was less and less gross, until eventually it became a craving.

As I got older, I stopped acting out homosexually, but I still watched gay porn occasionally. My addictions and compulsions got so bad that I flunked out of college twice. In college, I was a bit of a recluse. I would rather stay in my dorm room watching porn and masturbating than go to class, and eventually it caught up to me.

I grew up in a Christian home and always knew that pre-marital sex was wrong. The devil sold me this lie that watching porn and masturbating was better than actually having sex, and I bought it hook, line, and sinker. What I didn't realize, is that porn was actually driving me closer to sex. You can't feed that filth to your spirit and expect those seeds of lust not to produce fruit. It's inevitable. I started meeting women online through Craigslist and other online venues for anonymous, "no strings attached" sex. At least I thought there were no strings attached. I didn't realize then that I was creating soul ties with all of these women. I was giving them a part of me that I could never take back.

By the time I met my future wife, I had been with more than thirty women, and I carried all of that baggage into our relationship. My addictions nearly cost me my marriage before it even happened. Thankfully God sent me a wakeup call. I had an epiphany of sorts. He showed me the blueprint for breaking free from the kind of sexual bondage and addictions that had bound me for most of my life. In fact, I wrote a book about my experience. It's called *Something Greater: The Blueprint for Overcoming Sexual Addictions*. One of the foundational principles of the book is that God gave us our sex drives. It is not a nasty or dirty thing. However, he also gave us a steering wheel and brakes to help control that drive, just like a normal car. Our steering wheel is His Word. Your car has ABS brakes, which means anti-lock braking system. We too have ABS brakes for our sex drive. ABS = Arrest your thoughts. Bounce your eyes. Starve your flesh.

Everything that I've gone through has not been in vain. I've been walking in sexual purity now for four years; no porn, no masturbation, no lust. And I've been happily married to the best wife a guy could ask for four years. I don't brag about my past because I'm proud of it. I brag about it because I want you to know that there is hope. I crawled out of the gutter and made it to the top of the mountain, and if I can do it, so can you. If it's important to you, you'll find a way. If it's not, you'll find an excuse. Selah.

<u>Confession</u>: By Jean-Yves Gnoumou

I got saved when I was ten years old and I was very active in my church youth group. I learned how to develop a personal relationship with the Lord when I was a teenager and by age fifteen I had a pretty good understanding of sexual purity. Unfortunately, when I turned sixteen, I started to get physically involved with girls. At the beginning, it was just kissing and touching and it slightly progressed into "fingering" and oral sex. At the time, I thought it was ok as long as there was no actual intercourse. So I continued into those practices throughout high school, dating one girl after another. When I turned nineteen, I had my first sexual encounter with a girl that I was very much in love with. Back in the day, I was convinced that she was going to be my wife and I thought that it was ok for me to go all the way with her. Then, we broke up and I went off to college where I had several other sexual encounters. I was going to church every Sunday, praying often but I was still living in fornication. My whole perspective on sexual purity started changing only by the end of 2008, when my desire to get close to God grew. At the time, I was in a serious relationship and was sexually active with my girlfriend. However, every time we were being intimate I experienced "guilt" that became intolerable. I told her that I wanted us to stop being sexually active because of that "guilt" that I had in my heart. She could not understand my decision and our relationship started to deteriorate as I was becoming thirstier for God. My desire to dwell in His presence was getting stronger every day and being sexually active was becoming more painful than enjoyable. I eventually stopped that relationship and decided to live in sexual purity. It's been three years already that I have been trying really hard to walk in sexual purity. It is an ongoing battle but I no longer have that "guilt" in my heart. Now, I can freely come before GOD's and enjoy his presence. I recently started a new relationship with a beautiful woman who also has the desire to walk in sexual purity. I feel much better about our relationship to the point where I feel that GOD has my back. That feeling is so awesome and I am intending to live in sexual purity until I get married and enjoy sex to the fullest with my wife.

The Best Sex of My Life

"And now, you may kiss the very bone of your bone, the very flesh of your flesh. Now, you may kiss your bride!" Pastor Mike, spoke these words at the very end of our wedding ceremony, and it was all so surreal. It was unbelievable that it was all happening. Our lips touched for the first time. It was nice. It was exciting, but so many people were watching. (Don't laugh.) I was a little bit nervous, in a good way. Of course, following the ceremony was the reception. October 30, 2010 was the most beautiful autumn day of the year. The weather was absolutely gorgeous. I remember stepping out of the limo, approaching the reception to enter the most beautifully decorated ballroom, I'd ever seen. Gareth and I danced into the room to the tune of the *Black Eyed Peas* singing, "I got a feeling, that tonight's gonna be a good night, tonight's gonna be a good night, tonight's gonna be a good, good night." We were ecstatic, while our friends and family cheered us on like we were their favorite football team and had just won the Super bowl. It was the greatest feeling. We made it! We did it! It was hard at times, but it was worth it! Then, we danced to our song, *"Don't Change"* by Musiq Soulchild. From the tossing of the bouquet, the cutting of the cake, to the special tributes given by our family and friends, it was an unforgettable experience. It was a phenomenal day, but it wasn't over just yet! We left the reception, headed for the Ritz Carlton, on our way to Punta Cana, Dominican Republic and Cabo San Lucas, Mexico for the next two weeks. What would happen next for this newlywed couple is rated-X and sexually explicit!!!!!! Oh yea!! But seriously, we embarked on the exciting journey of the best sex of our lives! Every kiss and every touch was exciting and new. Our wedding night was priceless. Proverbs says:

91

> There are three *things which* are too wonderful for
> me, yes, four *which* I do not understand: The way of
> an eagle in the air, the way of a serpent on a rock,
> the way of a ship in the midst of the sea, and the
> way of a man with a virgin.
>
> Proverbs 30:19

Gareth was patient, gentle and loving with this virgin. We mutually enjoyed the new rewards, benefits and pleasures of sex, just the way God intended it. On October 30, 2010, the two became one flesh. We were naked and unashamed and God continues to be glorified!

Gareth and I received excellent counseling from our premarital counselors, and a great portion of their of their advice, knowledge and wisdom was given to us solely regarding sex, foreplay, intimacy, pleasing one another and enjoying this gift from God. God created sex! He created it for our pleasure, for our enjoyment and our delight! He created it, uniquely and solely, for a man and a woman committed to one another for life, in a covenant called marriage.

> Marriage is honorable among all, and the bed is
> undefiled; but fornicators and adulterers God will
> judge.
>
> Hebrews 13:4 (NKJV)

> Honor marriage, and guard the sacredness of sexual
> intimacy between wife and husband. God draws a
> firm line against casual and illicit sex.
>
> Hebrews 13:4 (MSG)

The Common English Bible quotes the same scripture saying:

> Marriage must be honored in every respect, with
> no cheating on the relationship, because God will
> judge the sexually immoral person and the person
> who commits adultery.
>
> Hebrews 13:4 (CEB)

From the scriptures, it is clear that we are to honor, respect and maintain the sanctity of marriage, regardless of the divorce rate, the current debate over same-sex marriages, the prominence of adultery or the rise of 'swingers'. Gareth and I have learned to honor our vows before God, and protect our sexual purity within marriage, because the enemy seeks to steal, kill and destroy us on this side of the relationship, just as he did in our single state. One night we went to a Japanese steakhouse, and we were seated with an interesting group of people. They began to indirectly proposition us to see if we would be interested in attending their 'swingers' event. Honestly, we were shocked but realized such behavior is commonplace in our generation. Do you think men have stopped trying to holler at me, or get my attention, just because I have a wedding ring on my finger? Whatever! They could care less. Moreover, for some, the wedding ring of a married man or woman is an incentive to pursue, even the more. My point is this: our goal for sexual purity didn't just disappear once we said "I do", but rather it increased and intensified. Now, we must guard our marriage from adultery, divorce, pornography, swingers and the like. At the same time, we have a duty to one another to keep our sex life on point. Keep it fresh! Keep it hot! Keep it sexy!

Understanding the difference between love and lust is important. It's important for a successful married sex life, but it is also important for living a focused single life. Lust, as defined by Dictionary.com, is an intense sexual desire or appetite. By definition, it is *uncontrolled* or *illicit* sexual desire. It seeks to fulfill its *uncontrolled, illicit* appetite at the expense of another. Sexual love, by contrast, will seek to fulfill the sexual desire of its spouse. Lust does not prepare you for sexual intimacy in marriage, in fact, it does just the opposite. Understanding that lust doesn't just depart from one's life after they say "I do" in marriage, explains why some people have trouble in their 'married sex lives'. If a man is consumed with the desire to be pleasured, satisfied and sexually fulfilled, with no concern for the pleasure, satisfaction or fulfillment of his new wife, this mentality can quickly lead to marital discord and extra-marital relationships. The selfish, self-centered desire to be pleasured, satisfied and sexually fulfilled above all things can destroy a marriage. Yes, men NEED sex and women NEED affection according to the relationship experts, but lust is far different from the basic NEED of sex. Both parties within the marriage relationship deserve to be fulfilled, and both parties within the relationship need to make the satisfaction of the other person, a top priority. Lust is self-centered. Lust is unquenchable. Therefore, a faithful husband or a faithful wife is no competition for a spouse consumed with lust.

Gareth and I purposed within our hearts to rid ourselves of all lust, and to make each other's sexual satisfaction a top priority. My heart was set on pleasing my husband and his heart was set on pleasing me, sexually. I speak candidly here, because many people asked me why I was not marrying another virgin. Some people felt very strongly that I should marry a male virgin. My vision clearly stated that I wanted a man who was 'a virgin in his heart, toward me and a virgin in his heart toward God'. In other words, when I met Gareth, although he was not a virgin physically, he was what the Apostle Paul referred to in 1 Corinthians 5:17 as a "new creature". The word 'new' in this context means new, unused or fresh. In spite of the women of his sexual past, he was now a new creature in Christ and all old things had passed away, according to the scripture, and all things had become new. We purposed within our hearts not to judge and compare one another to people from our past relationships, specifically he also pledged not to compare me to women from his sexual past. "Hit it & Quit it" sex, "Friends with Benefits" sex, "I Got Drunk and Oops" sex and "Serial Monogamy" is far different from the sexual intimacy, sanctity and spiritual oneness of the covenant marriage bed. Gareth and I made a clear decision early in our relationship not to allow the things of the past to corrupt what God ordained for our future.

The scriptures state:

> Now, getting down to the questions you asked in your letter to me. First, is it a good thing to have sexual relations? Certainly, but only within a certain context. It's good for a man to have a wife, and for a woman to have a husband. Sexual drives are strong, but marriage is strong enough to contain them and provide for a balanced and fulfilling sexual life in a world of sexual disorder. The marriage bed must be a place of mutuality, the husband seeking to satisfy his wife, the wife seeking to satisfy her husband. Marriage is not a place to 'stand up for your rights'. Marriage is a decision to serve the other, whether in bed or out.
>
> 1 Corinthians 7: 1-5 (MSG)

In other words, I seek to please my husband and he seeks to please me. I will expand on the more sexual aspects of this conversation in my next book, *The Best Sex of My Life: a Sexual Guide for a New Bride (& Groom)*. However, for the purpose of describing how much God celebrates sexual love and intimacy in the covenant of marriage, I will give you these references:

> Enjoy the wife you married as a young man! Lovely as an angel, beautiful as a rose, don't quit taking delight in her body. Never take her love for granted! Why would you trade enduring intimacies for cheap thrills with a whore or dalliance with a promiscuous stranger?
>
> Proverbs 5:18-20 MSG

> As a loving deer and a graceful doe, let her breasts satisfy you at all times; And always be enraptured with her love.
>
> Proverbs 5:19 NKJV

The sweet, fragrant curves of your body, the soft, spiced contours of your flesh invite me, and I come. I stay until dawn breathes its light and night slips away. You're beautiful from head to toe, my dear love, beautiful beyond compare, absolutely flawless. Come with me from Lebanon, my bride. Leave Lebanon behind, and come. Leave your high mountain hideaway. Abandon your wilderness seclusion, where you keep company with lions and panthers guard your safety. You've captured my heart, dear friend. You looked at me, and I fell in love. One look my way and I was hopelessly in love! How beautiful your love, dear, dear friend, far more pleasing than a fine, rare wine, your fragrance more exotic than select spices. The kisses of your lips are honey, my love, every syllable you speak a delicacy to savor. Your clothes smell like the wild outdoors, the ozone scent of high mountains. Dear lover and friend, you're a secret garden, a private and pure fountain. Body and soul, you are paradise, a whole orchard of succulent fruits, ripe apricots and peaches, oranges and ears; nut trees and cinnamon, and all scented woods; mint and lavender, and all herbs aromatic; A garden fountain, sparkling and splashing, fed by spring waters from the Lebanon mountains. Wake up, north wind, get moving south wind! Breathe on my garden, fill the air with spice fragrance. Oh, let my lover enter his garden! Yes, let him eat the fine, ripe fruits.

Song of Solomon 4:6-16

Yes, this text is from the Bible!!!

On October 30, 2010, God honored His promise to me. *"The Best Sex of My Life"* journey began, as I experienced sexual intimacy with my husband, Gareth on the night of our wedding; the journey continues. Our relationship is a modern-day Song of Solomon. Before we got married, the Lord clearly told me that no secular sexual encounter could compare to the sacred sexual encounter He ordained for my marriage. That's why I entitled my book series, *"The Best Sex of My Life"*. I knew God wanted his sons and daughters to experience the best. Any sexual encounter outside of the will of God pales in comparison to what the Lord has described as "the garden of delight" and being "naked and unashamed" (Genesis 2:25). God, being the original author, designer, and creator of sex can only be fraudulently copied by Satan, the imposter. That's why cheap, casual sex, adulterous affairs, 'one night stands', 'down-low' sexual encounters, Facebook sex, high school/college sex and cheap workplace sex usually leave people with shame, regret, bad memories and unfortunate consequences. The Lord mercifully spared me from a lot of drama, and on October 30, 2010 a beautiful, new and exciting chapter of my life began. A brand new world or lingerie, lubricants and love was opened up to me. We began to engage, enjoy, experiment and experience *'the best sex of my life'* journey. We were naked and unashamed!

I boldly write this because you need to know that God will honor you, when you honor Him. You need to understand that God is faithful and He is a rewarder of those who diligently seek Him (Hebrews 11:6). He will bless your marriage. He will bless your sex life. Happy marriages do exist. Great sex exists in happy marriages and yours will be one of them, one day. God created sex and He created the orgasmic pleasure of sex for a husband and wife to experience with one another; to bind, to tie, to unite and to connect them. That night we consummated our marriage covenant, I gave my virginity to my husband as a gift and the rest gets better and better!! (In my next book, *The Best Sex of My Life: a Sexual Guide for a New Bride (& Groom)* I will discuss the transition from sexual purity in singlehood to enjoyable sexual intercourse in marriage.)

In conclusion, I wanted to share this special poem Gareth composed for me and read at my bridal shower in September 2010. God is so faithful and if I had to do it all over again, I absolutely would. All of it was truly WORTH THE WAIT!!! I encourage you not to faint, not to quit and not to give up on this journey. God desires to cause your dreams to come true and give you the desires of your heart. Even as you are reading this book, He is perfecting the things that concern YOU, just like He did it for me (Psalm 138:8). My name is Lindsay Marsh Warren; these are my confessions, and I WAS WORTH THE WAIT!

Here's What You Bring . . .
By: Gareth Warren

Happiness that's better than the rest, Bringing God's
best to a man who stood the test of time,
Crime, grime and all other adversity set to bring a man down.
I'm thankful to God for trusting me with you . . .
His daughter, His jewel, a diamond in the light, never in the rough
My lady, my baby, my future wife,
You bring a value that's indefinable and for this I am grateful . . .
You never cease to amaze me in your ability to
motivate and inspire . . . YOU INSPIRE ME!
Ambitious but kind-hearted with a strong
desire to live hard . . . for God that is,
Your heart toward others, example to family & friends,
Anointing to decree God's word with boldness
and confidence and never wavering,
You represent the epitome of pleasing God.
For me you bring laughter, fun, joy and a commitment for life,
You can only imagine the happiness you bring to my life,
I am in love with your heart, your desire to please God,
And your thirst for a happy marriage that I stand firmly with you on,
You are my best friend . . . bringing a swaggocity
to the role of fiancée & friend,
And I know you will be a swaggalicious wife (wink)
I can't wait to say "Honey I'm home" or surprise
you with trips to exotic places
Or simple relaxing hideaways to recharge, rejuvenate,
and have indelible romantic days, nights & moments

With all you bring I want to give you more than you
deserve as your Godly husband . . . and I WILL!
35 days to go . . . we are almost at the starting line,
Keep holding my hand and looking toward God,
We are about to embark on a journey to set an
example of marriage to glorify God,
*And if you were wondering, the best sex of **our***
life is more than a one-night event,
It gets better and better and better and
better and better each time . . .
I LOVE YOU LINS!!!

Restoration

Merriam-Webster defines restoration as, "an act of restoring or the condition of being restored, a bringing back to a former position or condition, a restoring to an unimpaired or improved condition. Something that is restored; *especially*: a representation or reconstruction of the original form." We all have need of restoration. The need for restoration is a reality because none of us are perfect. When I was single, people would always ask me, ". . . since you are a virgin, do you want to marry a virgin?" My response would be 'no, not particularly'. This would usually shock the person. It wasn't because I had anything against marrying a 'male virgin'; I was indifferent. However, I understood that simply being a 'virgin' (physically) didn't necessary make you a person who embraced sexual purity. There are many perverted so-called, virgins. How do I know? I used to be one of them. I was physically a virgin, but many years ago I participated in 'satisfaction without penetration', entertained lustful thoughts, masturbation and things that did not honor God or my body. So, let me be clear; restoration is for all of us. Moreover, the precious blood of Jesus Christ is sufficient to cleanse us and purge us of anything and everything, according to Hebrews 9:14. You have to believe that and have faith in the Blood. Now is the time to be free from all of your past mistakes. I have faith in the blood of Jesus Christ. This same blood allowed Gareth and I the privilege to stand at the wedding altar of God, pure and white as snow. We stood at the altar, free from sin, free from condemnation, free from our past mistakes and free from our past relationships because of our faith in the blood of Jesus Christ. Jesus was our substitute and replacement on the cross. He took our place. He endured the punishment that was intended for us, and therefore, we refused to let His sacrifice be in vain. Do you recognize that you don't have to be tormented in your mind or by your past?

Please do yourself a favor and stop harboring feelings of self-hatred, low-self esteem, frustration and depression. Let it go. Cast your cares unto the Lord, for He cares for you (1 Peter 5:7). Suicide and self-mutilation is not the answer. "Cutting" won't solve your problems. Drowning out your issues with alcohol, marijuana or other recreational drugs will only compound the guilt, shame and heaviness. The enemy comes to destroy your life, but Jesus has come to give you life and a fresh start (John 10:10). Your fresh start begins with repentance. It begins with your confession. You have read about my confessions and the confessions of others in this book, but now it's time for you to make your own confession. 1 John 1:9 states, "If we confess our sins, he is faithful and just to forgive us our sins, and to cleanse us from all unrighteousness." Have you heard the saying that confession is good for the soul? Well, quite frankly, it's absolutely imperative to your spiritual well-being to know that you can go to a loving Father who cares for you, has a plan for you, adores you and welcomes you. Hebrews 4:16 says, "Let us therefore come boldly unto the throne of grace, that we may obtain mercy, and find grace to help in time of need." The same scripture in the Message Bible makes God's love and acceptance for us, clear:

> Now that we know what we have—Jesus, this great
> High Priest with ready access to God—let's not let it
> slip through our fingers. We don't have a Priest who
> is out of touch with our reality. He's been through
> weakness and testing, experienced it all—all but the
> sin. So let's walk right up to Him and get what He is
> so ready to give. Take the mercy, accept the help.
> Hebrews 4:16

The Lord desires to bring you back to your former position and condition. When He said in Genesis 1:26, "Let Us make (YOUR NAME GOES HERE), in Our image, after Our likeness: and let them have dominion . . ." God has designed you to dominate, to take charge, to rule and to have authority. You have authority over sin. You have authority over every generational curse. The sins of your father and mother have no control over you, because through the restoration by the blood of Jesus, you have dominion over all of these things. If I were to insert my name into this scripture, to make it personal to my situation, it would read, "Let Us make Lindsay, in Our image, after Our likeness: and let her have dominion . . ." He wants to restore you to a place of dominion.

Restoration is a journey, as well as a process that occurs by His grace, but it also requires that we make better choices. I want to take this opportunity to revisit a few principles I shared in *The Best Sex of My Life: a Guide to Purity* and earlier in this book. Again, if you are not familiar with my lesson, "10 Choices To Keep You Out of Trouble", I would recommend obtaining a copy, just to gather a better understanding of these choices.

1) Guard your heart (Proverbs 4:20-23)

2) Honor your parents, Pastors and mentors (Ephesians 6:2-3)

3) Hang with people who have your answer and get away from people who have your problem (1 Corinthians 15:33, Proverbs 12:26, Proverbs 13:20)

4) Pursue sexual purity (1 Thessalonians 4:3-8)

5) Build your self-esteem around the Word of God (Psalms 139:14-16, 1 Peter 2:9)

6) Go to church, Bible study and sessions that promote your spiritual growth (Hosea 4:6, Romans 12:2)

7) Get a vision for every area of your life: your mate, your education, your profession, your future, your ministry etc . . . (Proverbs 29:18, Habakkuk 2:2-4)

8) Pray consistently (Romans 8:26)

9) Change your attitude (Walk in love) (1 Corinthians 13:4-11)

10) Stop the sin (1 Corinthians 15:34, 1 John 1:9)

These ten choices were the foundation of my personal restoration and walking out that restoration on a day-to-day basis. These decisions allowed me to experience a consistent state of restoration. My Pastor, Dr. Michael A. Freeman, always says that "life is choice-driven, and you will live or die by the choices that you make." I encourage you to make better choices now that you have read the testimonies of those who have been sent to encourage, challenge and sharpen you. I admonish you to make choices that will honor the Lord and allow God to bring you His best. God wants to bless you with the mate of your dreams. He also wants you to be prepared to receive that person, as a blessing and not a burden; a blessing and not a distraction. I know this. Recognize the season you are in, and make decisions that will bring you closer to Him, rather than push God further away. He is a rewarder of those who diligently seek Him (Hebrews 11:6).

As I stated earlier, it is not by coincidence that you are reading this book. I believe that God assigned this book to you, as a pivotal transition into your maturity, development and restoration. I write from the purity of my heart to honor God and fulfill the call of God on my life, and I truly believe that you are reading this book because the Lord has called you to a new level of purity; purity of spirit, soul and body. I'm not referring to a superficial, 'people-pleasing', 'everything-looks-good-on-the-outside purity', but rather a 'no-faking', 'keep-it-real' purity that this generation desperately needs to see. We are the answer to the issues within our society and we are the answer to the issues within our families, communities and schools. We are the answer to the sexual challenges in our churches. As you and I walk in the manifestation of our restoration, we become the catalyst to change our world, one relationship at a time. You are a critical part of the Worth The Wait Revolution, as we are each modern day living epistles read of men, and people read our lives every day. Thank you for joining this REVOLUTION and completing this book and for adding your name to the list of those who have been impacted by this message. I encourage you to read and sign the sexual purity confession covenant at the conclusion of this book. Commit to this journey. Commit to this lifestyle. Commit to a rewarding experience of pleasing God. Together, let's revolutionize this generation with a life-changing message of real sexual purity as we each share our own personal journeys of overcoming by the blood of the Lamb and by the word of our very own testimony (Revelation 12:11)!

Confession For a Relationship

Dear God in Heaven, I come to You in the name of Jesus. Your Word says, "Whoever shall call on the name of the Lord shall be saved" (Acts 2:21). Lord, I call on you. I pray and ask Jesus to come into my heart and be Lord over my life. According to Romans 10:9-10, "If you shall confess with your mouth the Lord Jesus and believe in your heart that God has raised Him from the dead, you shall be saved". Lord, I do this right now. I confess that Jesus is Lord and I believe in my heart that You, God, raised Him from the dead. I am saved. You are now, my Heavenly Father and I am a child of the Most-High God.

In the name of Jesus. Amen!

Sexual Purity
Confession Covenant

I, _____, agree to pursue sexual purity as an act of my will. Sexual purity is my personal choice. Therefore, daily, I will make choices that help cultivate and establish the perfect will of God for my life, because I deserve God's best!

I will adhere to the principles I have learned from the Word of God.

1) I choose to guard my heart. I will be mindful of the things I allow myself to be exposed to; from music to movies to videos, I will be selective about what I allow to influence my thinking and decision-making. (Proverbs 4:21-23)

2) I choose to honor my parents, Pastors and mentors, by submitting to godly authority and godly advice. I understand that these people are a part of God's 'protection plan' for my life. (Ephesians 6:2-3)

3) I choose to hang with people who have my answer, and get away from people who have my problem. (Pastor Mike's Motto) I understand that the companion of fools will be destroyed, so I choose my friends and associates carefully. (1 Corinthians 15:33, Proverbs 12:26, and 13:20)

4) I choose to pursue a life of sexual purity. My body is the temple of God. I respect, honor and esteem this temple. I will not defile or abuse it in any way. Therefore, I avoid and turn away from all sexual sin: premarital sex, homosexuality, masturbation, oral sex, 'humping' and/or anything similar! (1 Thessalonians 5:22, Romans 8:14, 1 Corinthians 6:12)

5) I choose to build my self-esteem around the Word of God. I am complete in Christ Jesus. My money, my cars, my real estate, my accomplishments, my athletic ability, my positions, my titles, my clothes, my jewelry, and my girlfriend/boyfriend do not 'make' me! The Word of God has established my self-esteem. I am a chosen generation, a royal priesthood and a holy nation. I am fearfully and wonderfully made. I like me! (1 Peter 2:9, Colossians 2:9, Psalms 139:14-16)

6) I choose to come to church, bible study and other sessions that promote spiritual growth, because I must stay on the cutting edge of learning and development with my relationship with God. I keep my mind renewed so that I can fulfill the perfect will of God for my life. (Hosea 4:6, Romans 12:1-2)

7) I choose to be a person with vision. I release my faith for God's best in my future mate, my professional goals, my destiny and my dreams. I choose to remain focused so I will not make decisions I will regret later in life. (Habakkuk 2:2-4, Proverbs 29:18)

8) I choose to pray consistently. I have a relationship with God. I talk to Him about the big things, as well as, the little things. In everything, I acknowledge Him, including male/female relationships. He answers me and makes my path straight and clear. (Jeremiah 33:3)

9) I choose to change my attitude, and walk in the love of God. I have divorced myself from comparison and competition. I have divorced myself from a rebellious attitude. I have divorced myself from being arrogant, prideful and obnoxious. Now that I am mature, I have put away immature things. (1 Corinthians 13)

10) I choose to stop the sin in my life. As an act of my will, I repent and turn away from any activity that does not honor God and my body. I am stronger, I am greater, and I am bigger, than any temptation, test or trial that comes my way, because the Greater One lives on the inside of me. (1 Corinthians 15:34)

I am fully restored and renewed by the blood of Jesus, regardless of my past errors or mistakes. I have a fresh start, in Christ Jesus!

I choose to keep myself sexually pure until the day that I marry God's best for my life! Therefore, I fully expect and anticipate for God, my Father, to give me the desires of my heart because I have followed His instruction. On my wedding day, I fully expect and anticipate *THE BEST SEX OF MY LIFE!*

In the name of Jesus, my lifestyle is an excellent example for others to follow!!

_____

Signature and date

_____

Witness Signature and date

About The Author

Dr. Lindsay Marsh Warren is inspiring this generation to desire a sexual purity swag that redefines the meaning of abstinence. Originally from Shaker Heights, Ohio, Lindsay attended The George Washington University in Washington, D.C. for undergraduate, medical school, and post-graduate training, specializing in anesthesiology.

Upon moving to Washington, DC at the age of 18, she connected with her awesome Pastors, Drs. Michael and DeeDee Freeman of the Spirit of Faith Christian Center.

Dr. Lindsay was chosen as an Early Selection Honoree for the School of Medicine, and therefore exempt from taking the national qualifying exam, the MCAT. Yielding to the call of God on her life, she was ordained at the age of 21, and became a physician at the age of 25. Married at 34, she boldly shares her journey of maintaining her virginity until marriage, in her first book, *The Best Sex of My Life: A Guide To Purity*. Her second book, *The Best Sex of My Life: Confessions of A Sexual Purity Revolution*, discusses dating, courtship and engagement topics, while featuring the testimonies of those who have been impacted by the Revolution. It furthers the discussion on sexual purity after abortion, abuse, homosexuality, divorce, promiscuity and more. She has been featured on CNN's *Young People Who Rock*, BET's *Lift Every Voice*, NPR's *Tell Me More with Michelle Martin*, Gospel Today Magazine, W.H.U.R. Howard University Radio's *The Daily Drum* and The Washington Post. Additionally, she has been a featured speaker/panelist at various conferences, colleges, high schools, churches and events.

Her non-profit, *Worth The Wait Revolution, Inc.* is an organized movement of sexual purity that is the counter-culture to the sexploitation of our day. Dr. Lindsay and Worth The Wait Revolution host their annual Gala, Runway Events, and more to promote the theme of 'sexual purity with contemporary style and urban class'.

Her t-shirt lines, "I AM WORTH THE WAIT", "HE WAS WORTH THE WAIT" and "SWAGGSTINENT" are revolutionizing the mindset of this generation. October 30, 2010, in an amazingly gorgeous wedding, she was married as a virgin, to her handsome husband, Gareth P. Warren. Their first kiss took place on their wedding day. Together, they are declaring a transparent message of sexual purity and restoration to the nations, for men and women, alike.

Lindsay is greatly humbled and appreciative of God's blessing and favor on her life and accepts the challenge of being a 'supermodel' for the kingdom of God. She gives God all the glory and credits her success to Him, her parents and her Pastors.

Lindsay Marsh Warren, MD
Worth The Wait Revolution, Inc.
P.O. Box 1234
Temple Hills, Maryland 20757-1234
301-505-5000
www.iamworththewait.com
president@iamworththewait.com

To book Dr. Lindsay M. Warren for a *speaking engagement*, please email or call us using the contact information stated above.

To book the *Worth The Wait Revolution Runway Tour* to come to your conference, school, church or event, please email or call us using the contact information stated above.

Bulk orders available upon request

To purchase your soft cover book or MP3 audio book of *The Best Sex of My Life: A Guide To Purity*, please visit: www.iamworththewait.com

To purchase your *"I AM WORTH THE WAIT"* or *"HE WAS WORTH THE WAIT"* shirt, please visit: www.iamworthewait.com

To purchase your *"SWAGGstinent"* shirt (black), please visit: www.iamworththewait.com

To purchase your "WORTH THE WAIT REVOLUTION" wristbands, please visit: www.iamworththewait.com

To purchase your "10 Choices To Keep You Out of Trouble" bookmarks, 'Official' Sexual Purity Covenant Confession certificates, and more please visit: www.iamworththewait.com

Please add $4.99 for shipping & handling to all orders.

Name: _____

Shipping Address:_____

City/State/Zip: _____

Billing Address: _____

City/State/Zip: _____

Contact Number: _____ Contact Email: _____

Credit Card Number: _____

Security Code (3-digits): _____

Products for Purchase: _____

(Please specify color and quantity, if applicable). Make checks payable Worth The Wait, LLC and send to the address above.